The GARDF
REDEMPTION

by

WILLIAM E. ROYDEN

Robert M. McBride & Company
NEW YORK   1927

THE GARDEN OF REDEMPTION

CONTENTS

THE GARDEN OF REDEMPTION

The GARDEN *of* REDEMPTION

Chapter I

Mr. Herbertson Meets a May Morning

THAT Second of May opened with conspicuous charm and without a hint of tragedy. Mr. Herbertson awoke at six-thirty to realise that he had had a dreamless night, and that his garden was calling through his open window with many voices. He rose at once, for though he was not a man of action he had no use for idle reverie. Like a bad dream, it was apt to set the old ghosts walking.

During Spring and Summer he usually spent an hour in his garden before breakfast. He put on, therefore, an old Norfolk suit, plentifully soil-stained, and then spent a minute at the window, looking out upon the domain which was his refuge and his pride. His bedroom and his study both looked out upon the garden, and the bedroom window was a large bay of his own design.

A glance at his garden usually gave him keen pleasure, and to-day its beauty might have been apparent even to the most insensitive of men. It was the beauty of Spring and of morning, the beauty

9

of blossom and of fruit, the beauty of sure, inevitable growth, the beauty of song and of silence, the beauty of fulfilment, and expectation, and peace. Mr. Herbertson realised it all, for he was a true artist in spirit. But the garden called him clearly, so he opened the window wider, to air the room, and went downstairs.

His housekeeper, Mrs. Jenner, had gone down a few minutes before, and he could hear her movements in the kitchen. From a stand in the hall he took an old tweed hat which was even older than his gardening suit, and then went into the room which he called his study. There on his writing table stood a Shakespeare calendar, and it was one of his habits to begin each day by bringing this useful and interesting device up to date. He never forgot this little duty, and there was no reason why he should forget it now. Indeed, the beauty of the morning called for an appropriate thought in beautiful words, and he wondered if the calendar would be equal to the occasion.

It did its best, but he could not see that the result was happy. When he tore off the slip with his usual care he came upon familiar lines which had nothing to do with gardens:

Things base and vile, holding no quantity
Love can transpose to form and dignity;
Love looks not with the eyes but with the mind,
And therefore is winged Cupid painted blind.

Mr. Herbertson immediately found the key-word of the lines. "Transpose," he murmured. "Now I wonder what he really had in mind. The context suggests Love the Illusionist, making us take the Ass for a King: but the word itself carries more than that. It suggests Love the Miraculous, changing—actually changing—the Ass into the King. I must look into it—some day. . . . But whatever the content of that word, the lines are utterly unsuitable. . . . They have no application. They appeal to foolish youth, and have no message for the middle aged. . . . What I need is a post-Meridian Calendar."

He smiled as he threw yesterday's slip into a waste-paper basket, for the idea pleased him. Then he opened the door that led into the garden, and passed into the fresh air of the morning. As he did so he raised his head and squared his shoulders a little, and breathed deep; for on this May morning the old world throbbed and quivered with life, life that was bursting into leaf and flower and fruit; and as it enveloped the man who had just reached the point of middle-age, it bore him back for a moment into a realm of youth again, stirred his spirit to a sense of harmony with the world of Spring in which he stood.

It was only for a moment or two, for then he reflected that he was a Post-Meridian person. Quite as suddenly as it had come the impression passed, and he remembered that he was simply enjoying the first breath of a fine morning. He went on to a small outhouse, procured a hoe, and walked down the garden to the task he had appointed for the hour.

The house in which he lived was a small, semi-detached "villa" of eight rooms. His garden was divided from that of his neighbour by a wall, breast-high—a solid, mossy wall of brown stone, which often gave him unappreciative recollections of the tarred-board fences that divide the gardens of suburban London. The portion of garden that pertained to each house was fairly long but rather narrow, but Mr. Herbertson was not limited to this rule. He had added to his own a considerable piece of ground which ran behind his own house-plot and several others also, and this provided him with occupation for all the time he could give to it. Indeed, it had already outgrown his authority, and was a labyrinth of foliage and confusion that sadly needed the attention of an expert and pitiless gardener. Mr. Herbertson was not pitiless, and it was almost enough for him to survey that chaos from his windows and plan its reduction for some other day.

As for Mr. Herbertson himself, it may be said here that he was a very undistinguished citizen of Waldington. He had some private means, and owned this modest house in Arran Terrace, a leafy avenue of small, red-brick villas. He wrote a little both in prose and verse, but very inconspicuously; and he could use the brush with some skill, for his own amusement or that of his friends. At this time his age was forty-five, so that it was possible that he had a past; but his tastes and his occupations seemed to forbid the possibility of any future. It was a mere coincidence that Arran Terrace was a *cul-de-sac,* but the spot certainly owed some of its peace to the fact that there was no thoroughfare.

This morning he pottered about with his hoe for some time, to be aroused at last by the approach of his housekeeper. The early post had just passed, and she brought a letter, with the intimation that breakfast was ready. Mrs. Jenner was a silver-haired and comfortable woman of sixty, who was sensible enough to thank Heaven every day that her widowhood had found a shelter and an honourable task under Mr. Herbertson's roof.

"Good morning, Mrs. Jenner," said Mr. Herbertson. "It is a fine day."

"Yes," said the housekeeper. "And a fine washing day. And breakfast is just ready, sir."

Mr. Herbertson had forgotten that it was washing day, and he did not care for the news. As Mrs. Jenner turned away he examined the letter with a slightly sobered face. It bore the seal of a firm of seed merchants from which he had ordered certain garden supplies a few days before. He was expecting these supplies to-day, and this letter told him that the parcel would not reach him until to-morrow.

"Ah, well," he said. "I thought I should get that matter well forward to-day. One never knows."

He went slowly up towards the house until he reached the brown-stone wall of the kind he had never seen in suburban London. As he approached it he saw his next-door neighbour on the other side—a young man whose entirely suitable name was George Hadfield.

Hadfield saw Mr. Herbertson at the same moment. "Good morning," he said cheerily. "You have begun in good time."

Mr. Herbertson rested his hand on the wall. "Yes," he said. "But I cannot go on. The things I've ordered from Stoughton's haven't been sent. They won't come until to-morrow."

Hadfield was no gardener. It satisfied him to have his garden a "lawn," and his gardening consisted of keeping this lawn in fair condition with a small mower. He was a very ordinary young Englishman, large in build and easy of temper, with a brown skin, light hair, and a very boyish face. He stood in his shirt-sleeves, and was enjoying a morning pipe. To this day he cannot tell what were the supplies Mr. Herbertson referred to.

"That's unfortunate," he said cautiously. "But I suppose a day won't make much difference. Will it?"

"Difference? Oh, no," answered the elder man thoughtfully. "But I had arranged to attend to them to-day. That's all. One likes to carry out one's plans, you know."

Hadfield smiled. Though not of an observant disposition, he had often been amused to note his neighbour's methodical habits. It occurred to him to try to break the chain, and he proffered the suggestion which was to have such surprising results.

"Well," he said, "since you can't do that, why not something quite different? Why not take a day off? Why not—say—run up to town for a few hours?"

Waldington is only an hour from London, and reasonably well served by the Great Northern. Mr. Herbertson shook his head; but this was only the methodical man's instinctive shrinking from movements which had not been fully considered. The proposal had a strong advocate in the breath of that May morning, and he was considering it quite seriously when Mrs. Hadfield came out to join her husband.

This little lady was as dark as her husband was

fair, bright-eyed and clear-complexioned, and with neatness in every aspect and movement. Ten months of married life had brought her nothing but happiness, and her eyes reflected the sunshine which had its home in her heart. She regarded Mr. Herbertson as a friend, and he was that most interesting of all friends, a friend who is also a Problem. The eligible bachelor in the forties, who seems to care nothing for any woman in particular while he is delightfully courteous to woman in general—what more attractive Problem could any young matron wish to find next door? She greeted him archly now, with a smile and a question:

"What!" she said. "Gardening already?"

"He has been in his forest for the last hour," said her husband lazily. "But I have been advising him to take a day off, and run up to town."

"Ah," said Mrs. Hadfield with a sigh, and with eyes full of vision, "wouldn't that be delightful? Are you going? Just think of Regent Street on a morning like this!"

"And Peter Robinson's corner," murmured her husband.

Mr. Herbertson smiled. He found considerable enjoyment in these young people. They were a study for him, just as he in his sedate bachelordom was a study for them. At this moment he was making a mental note that Mrs. Hadfield was attired in a new housekeeping garment. It appeared to be of the nature of a pinafore or overall of some thin, washable material, and it suited her very well. When he reached this conclusion, some association of ideas led him to recall a picture which was indelibly impressed upon his memory—

the picture of a stout man who was a Registrar of Births and Deaths, and who was sitting stolidly at his duties in a dreary little wooden office, with his nether limbs encased in a pair of riding breeches! They had not suited him at all, and though the incident had occurred many years ago, Mr. Herbertson had failed to forget it. He often wondered why that Registrar had done such a thing, and whether other Registrars also were in the habit of doing it.

"Well," he said indulgently, "I'll think it over. Certainly the idea is worth considering. It is actually three years since I was in London."

"Three years!" exclaimed Mrs. Hadfield. "And only forty miles away!"

"Three years!" repeated her husband. "My word, Madge!"

Mr. Herbertson did not seem at all abashed, but it is probable that he took his resolve just at that instant. For a few moments they stood discussing the subject lightly, and then Mrs. Hadfield reminded her husband of the necessity of breakfast before he should depart for his duties at the offices of the Waldington Urban District Council. The company broke up, therefore, with smiles, and Mr. Herbertson went towards his own delayed meal.

Before he reached his breakfast, however, another item claimed place in his programme. At the head of his garden he glanced at his watch. It was twenty-three minutes to nine. Then he stood for three minutes, watch in hand, looking across the gardens towards the end of the Terrace: and just as the watch said twenty-to-nine, a head rose into his near horizon over the dividing wall of one of the neighbouring houses. As it rose, a clear call came across the space between:

"Coo-ee-ee!"

Mr. Herbertson answered adequately. The head steadied itself, and shoulders followed. A little girl of eight or so was standing on a small step-ladder and holding by one hand to a clothes-line post. She had a brown, chubby face with large eyes, and the short, thick, brown hair which hung curling to her neck was cut to a deep fringe on her forehead. She was graceful in figure, alto-gether a presentable maiden, and she wore a school suit of blue serge. Her school cap had a red but-ton on the top and a monogram badge in front.

After the first greeting a curious ceremony took place. Mr. Herbertson said "Good morning," and the child replied "Good morning." Then he raised his right hand with one finger pointing upwards. It was a code question, and the child answered it by pointing direct at Mr. Herbertson himself. Then another finger joined the first, making Ques-tion Number Two: and Margaret Joan Mead answered this by laying her right hand upon her heart.

"Whom do you love?"

"*You.*"

"How much?"

"*With all my heart.*"

Then Mr. Herbertson raised his indescribable garden hat with indescribable politeness, and the figure vanished from the wall. The ceremony was over, and another little schoolgirl was waiting for this one at the corner of Arran Terrace. As for

Mr. Herbertson, he strolled into his house and went to wash his hands for breakfast, obviously a gentleman of pleasant tastes and kindly ways, with some eccentric but not ungracious items in the programme of his life. But it was equally obvious, surely, that he was far removed from the type usually marked by Destiny for high and perilous adventure. This house and its garden matched him exceedingly well, and the Hadfields, Margaret Joan and Mrs. Jenner took their places in the scene with absolute naturalness.

During the course of his solitary breakfast he finally decided to adopt Hadfield's suggestion. Certainly this would be an excellent morning for Regent Street, Piccadilly and Hyde Park Corner. He knew how the town on a day like this would be full of colour and movement, how the very swing of its omnibuses would have a joyous cadence, how the motors would rush by with a shout and a song. He could have an easy day and be back in time for an hour or two of gardening at the end of it. Besides, he could make this an opportunity of attending to a trifling matter of business in London, and thus give his holiday some appearance of usefulness. It did not occur to him then that Mrs. Hadfield's overall had anything to do with his decision.

He finished his meal and went to find his housekeeper. "Mrs. Jenner," he said cheerfully, "I am going to run up to London, and you need not expect me back until to-night."

"Well, sir," said the old lady, "I'm glad to hear it. You ought to have a little change now and again, especially on a washing day—what with the woman in the house, and the steam all over the place, as it will get in spite of everything; and I'll have a nice meal ready for you when you come back."

"Very good," said Mr. Herbertson, smiling. "That will ensure my return."

He took half-an-hour to discard his garden costume, and then reappeared in another grey suit of much more recent purchase. In his study he glanced at an old time-table in order to verify the time of the train; and then he looked round, with the natural instinct of an orderly mind, to see that nothing was out of place.

Apparently there was nothing except the calendar. "The only incongruous item in this bachelor's apartment," said Mr. Herbertson lightly, "is that quotation! We will change it later!"

As he spoke he noticed that the author of the lines was looking at him steadily from the illuminated back of the calendar—the eyes of infinite humanity overshadowed by the tremendous brow of infinite knowledge. He was intrigued by that look. He imagined challenge in it, and in his whimsical way he answered the challenge.

"Yes, Wise One," he said, half aloud, "you have made a bad shot this time. But you shall try again to-morrow."

He thought he had said the final word on that subject, but it was not so. After he had gone the day was washing day, with a capable and careful woman in the scullery. As it was a light day she finished by noon, and Mrs. Jenner then brought her to the study to give it a careful polish during its master's absence. In dusting Mr. Herbertson's writing-table she moved the calendar and it slipped down behind the desk to the floor. This desk was a heavy one, made in three sections, so Mrs. Jenner refused to take the risk of moving it. After some cogitation she went into town in the afternoon and bought a new calendar as a substitute; but there were few calendars to be had in May, and the one she obtained had no quotations and had nothing to do with Shakespeare, though for the chief purpose of a calendar's existence it was equally good. "And if Mr. Herbertson doesn't like it," thought this excellent woman as she placed it in position, "well, it's for him to have the desk moved, to get the other. And I'll use this one in the kitchen."

When Mr. Herbertson came home he was duly informed of the incident, but there were good reasons for his lack of further interest in the matter. He adopted the substitute with a preoccupied "Thank you," and used it faithfully through the days that followed. Indeed, he had forgotten that inappropriate quotation altogether.

But the calendar lay behind the desk, and the Wise One who had been mocked held his peace down there in the dark and the dust, content to wait his time.

Chapter II

Mr. Herbertson Leaves His Garden

WHEN Mr. Herbertson reached the railway station he had ten minutes to spare. Haste had no place in his ordered life, and in his infrequent journeyings he regulated his movements as if every train started ten minutes before its schedule time. It was some two years since he had begun to build, in that forest of a garden, a greenhouse of spacious dimensions which should be entirely the work of his own hands; and the comfortable way in which he gave this *magnum opus* an afternoon now and again when the spirit moved him was to his neighbours a marvel and a study. His literary contributions to one or two magazines had breathed the same atmosphere, and were greatly enjoyed by readers of leisure and reflection.

When the train came in he secured an empty compartment, and spent the first fifteen minutes in reading a morning paper. After that he sat looking out upon the sunshine-flooded landscape with much of the enjoyment which a boy may find on his journey homeward for the holidays, though it did not find the same method of expression. Then came King's Cross, almost cheerful with the spirit of the spring morning, and the necessity of deciding what to do first.

Mr. Herbertson resolved that it must be business first, and walked out to the street. An omnibus bore him to Holborn, where he got down to make his way eastwards. A little later he was in Paternoster Row, seeking that House of Murchisons which has so long occupied its prominent position on its grimy corner. Even to-day the corner was grimy and the office gloomy, but there was certainly some reflection of the spirit of May in the smile of the clerk who took his card. Yes, Mr. MacArthur was in, and might be disengaged.

Mr. MacArthur was disengaged and in a good humour. He recalled the name of Mr. Herbertson, referred to certain records, and decided to see him. So Mr. Herbertson stepped upstairs to find May here also, responsible for the cordiality of a gentleman whose natural attitude was one of cautious enquiry with a background of suspicion.

"Ah, Mr. Herbertson," he said. "How do you do after these long years? Have you just come up?" For his visitor's air and attire spoke clearly of the country.

"Yes," said Mr. Herbertson, somewhat interested in his errand and the man, but more interested in the dark oak panelling of the room. "I have come straight from King's Cross."

"From the country—on a day like this? Then I suppose it is business?"

"It is really nothing of importance," explained the visitor. "But I thought I would call and enquire about my little book. I wondered whether —whether you would be thinking of a new edition, or anything of that kind. Or is it entirely dead?"

The publisher touched a bell, which brought a

clerk to the door. "Let me have a copy of Mr. James Herbertson's *Styrian Riddle*," he said; and during the interval of waiting he sought other matter for conversation.

"It is a lovely day," he remarked. "I suppose it tempted you out? But you come to London, whereas I should go to the country. Are you still at Waldington?"

"Yes."

"And have you published anything lately?"

"A little," answered Mr. Herbertson. "Essays and other trifles. I have a garden, you know."

Mr. MacArthur cast about mentally for the connection between the garden and the Essays. It did not occur to him that Mr. Herbertson only gave to literary work what attention he could spare from the garden.

"That sounds pleasant," he ventured. "Is it a large garden?"

"Respectably large. More than I can manage. That, of course, is the advantage of it. I have always a little more than I can do—which some philosophers have described as Happiness."

Mr. MacArthur smiled. He began to have an impression that he liked this visitor from the country, whom he had almost forgotten, and that he would like to see his garden. It was at this point that the clerk returned with the book—a small volume in a plain grey binding, but with a somewhat striking design upon the cover—an eagle perched on a pinnacle of rock, gazing skywards, daring the sun.

"Ah!" he said, "here it is: *The Styrian Riddle*. This is the second edition, issued at the time the

Emperor seemed to be dying. You wrote a fresh chapter on the Styrian situation at my request, did you not?"

Mr. Herbertson intimated that this was so. The publisher nodded.

"Well," he said, "I cannot say that I had thought of a new edition. In fact the second edition did not go off completely. There is still a small stock in the house. And things over there appear to be quieting down of late. They have a strong man at the head of affairs.—By the way, Baron Ronnefeldt does not appear in your story at all."

"No," said Mr. Herbertson. "At that time he hadn't emerged."

"Of course, of course. It is only a few years since he caught the attention of Europe by his handling of the Turks. A brilliant bit of work, that. . . . But do you think he will solve the Riddle? If so, there may be room for a brief biography."

"It is possible that he may solve the Riddle," said Mr. Herbertson. "But I hardly think I could write his story. I have been quite out of touch with Styria of late."

"I see. Well, the question of a new edition cannot be answered definitely just now. If it arises I will let you know, of course."

Mr. Herbertson did not seem grievously disappointed. Mr. MacArthur closed the book and glanced at the cover. "This design," he said, "the Styrian eagle, is it not? I am always a little uncertain about those eagles—the Russian, the Prussian, and the Styrian."

"Yes," said Mr. Herbertson. "That is the Styrian eagle—the emblem of the Salzburgs. And the present Emperor has done a little to justify his emblem."

"He has," agreed the publisher. "He is a very fine old man. Well, if anything should turn up I will communicate with you. One never knows. . . . But you said something just now about Essays. If you are making a collection of them, we might see it. Not that Essays are much of an investment at any time. But still—"

He smiled genially, still under the spell of May. "Thank you," said Mr. Herbertson. "I will certainly bear the matter in mind. Good morning, Mr. MacArthur."

They shook hands at the door, and Mr. Herbertson passed downstairs and out to the Row. The publisher returned to his seat, took up the little book, and turned the leaves thoughtfully till he came to a certain chapter. He remembered quite clearly now that the author's treatment of the unfortunate subject of this chapter was not only severe, but was even cruel. He could not reconcile this with the impression which Mr. Herbertson had made upon himself. The man who had treated another's failure in such a merciless spirit was gentle and courteous, with a kindly smile in his eyes and an evident love for his garden. But then the publisher remembered that Mr. Herbertson had once been intimately connected with that wretched scion of the Salzburgs—had been his secretary or something of the kind.

"He was probably disappointed," he thought; "it may be that they quarrelled. A man you have disappointed is hardly the man to write your epitaph. Yes, I suppose the secret lies just there.

Well, I think the man may write a good essay. We'll see." And with that he dismissed the matter from his mind.

In the meantime Mr. Herbertson had left the building. At the outer doors he paused, apparently to consider the results of the interview. Curiously enough, his expression did not at all suggest a disappointed author. It might have been one of pleasure and relief rather than disappointment.

"I think," he said, half aloud, as he stood for a moment on the doorstep, "I think I may consider that chapter closed. Closed!"

He turned to the right, and walked slowly up the Row. Once or twice he paused to gaze into a gaily decorated window, possibly with a vague recollection of his Post-Meridian Calendar: yet his thoughts were little concerned with what he saw in the windows of the Row.

"Dead long ago, and forgotten," he reflected. "Forgotten so far that we need only remember the fact of his death. There is not even any one to ask 'Where is he buried?' much less 'How did he die?'"

Now he had reached the end of the Row, and stood facing the entrance to Cheapside, with its stream of ceaseless traffic. For a while he stood irresolute, an idle, grey-clad figure stranded upon the kerb.

"Well," he thought, not without amusement, "I had intended to go to the west, and here I find myself with my face to the east. Now I wonder why I turned to the right when I came out of Murchisons', instead of to the left. It was quite involuntary. Could it be that I was drawn in this direction—that it was the influence of the man who was in my thoughts, and who lies out here forgotten?"

Across the street the omnibuses passed, coming out of Newgate Street and pausing there before continuing their journey. As he looked, one of them swung round to the corner and stopped. Mr. Herbertson stared, his random musings thrown into confusion. From its elevated place at the back of the 'bus a familiar name seemed to shout a challenge. That name was Maywood Park.

In his present mood Mr. Herbertson could only accept the challenge. Quite rapidly he crossed the street and approached the omnibus. "It is evident," he said to himself, "that I am invited to go out there to-day—perhaps to make sure that no one knows how the Prince died. I have nothing to do, and I have time. Why should I not go?"

Chapter III

—And Ventures Into a Field

THE immense cemetery of Maywood Park lies far eastward, and Mr. Herbertson reached it after a journey of some forty minutes. Even here the joy and stir of a spring morning brooded over all, and Nature was in the full tide of life over the green acres of the dead. Indeed, Mr. Herbertson had a curious fancy as he came up to the great iron gates which stood wide open. Those who had been laid to rest in their long-ranked mounds under the popular impression that they should stay there until the sound of the Great Trump—could it be that they also felt the thrill of the new life that was passing through the old world? Was it possible that the bonds might be broken, and that secrets and shames might rise out of their slumbers?

When he entered the grounds, however, this fancy was quickly put aside. There was life, but the lost army was not touched by it any more than it was moved by the shriek of the City trains that passed under the very shadow of its tombstones. The place was exceedingly still. One or two attendants were at work upon the grounds, and there were some half-dozen visitors within sight. Two of these came almost face to face with him as soon as he had passed in.

They were evidently mourners. One was a woman of mature age, closely veiled, and the other, upon whose arm she leaned heavily, appeared to be her daughter. Mr. Herbertson glanced at them with sympathetic but casual curiosity at first; but the character of his glance changed immediately, and became intent. It was a view of the younger woman's face that caused the change, for she chanced to look up as they passed. She looked directly at Mr. Herbertson, but not attentively, as though her thoughts were elsewhere.

The meeting was only momentary, for they had walked on; but it was sufficient to impress Mr. Herbertson. He was a worshipper of the beautiful, and it seemed to him that the face of the girl was strikingly attractive. Moreover, the cast of features gave him a curious impression of remembrance and recognition. Yet this impression must obviously be a false one.

"What vagrant fancies we get," he thought, "when we go out among strangers after a long period of home quiet! One's senses are all on the alert, as it were, and snatch many unreasonable impressions. I could have declared that I had met that girl before. It was the type, perhaps—the almost olive skin, with hazel eyes—"

He turned once to look after the couple, but they had already disappeared. Then, still musing upon this puzzling impression, he passed on into the grounds.

But although the second impression had been thrust away, the first remained with him. The girl had been exceedingly attractive, and for a man of middle-age there are few more interesting things in this world than a young and beautiful face. At this period, however, mere perfection of feature is not all that is looked for. There is a demand, or at least a desire, for the suggestion of a more satisfying beauty—that of mind and heart; and it was this that had appealed to him in the brief glance which he had caught.

Then he remembered the purpose of his visit to this place, and dismissed that casual encounter. With the remembrance came a return of his earlier humour. He walked on through the quiet pathways, looking idly to right and left, pausing now and again to examine one or other of the many monuments which stood near his path. He seemed to be looking for a name which he should recognise, but there was no urgency in his search and no anxiety. As a matter of fact he was not looking for a name, but for a number. Many of the mounds had a numbered stake planted at the foot, but the numbers he saw did not approach the one he had in mind.

"I could not forget it," he said. "I remember too well how that white-bearded old undertaker handed it to me on a slip of paper as soon as the affair was properly over. The fool—if he had only known how little I wanted to have the thing! But I looked at it unawares, and afterwards found it impossible to forget 12784. Nothing more than a number like that in a place like this! What a climax to a career—a Career!—and the dream of a Crown! . . . I am afraid I have entirely forgotten the direction. And, no doubt, the place has changed a good deal since that day."

Then he saw an attendant some distance off,

engaged in cutting the grass on a stretch of yet undisturbed ground. Mr. Herbertson looked at his watch.

"Perhaps he will be able to direct me," he said, half aloud. "Yet I am afraid that it is scarcely worth while to ask him. When a man is quite forgotten, why trouble to find his grave?"

Smiling a little at his thoughts, he returned his watch to its place; but he had now decided to pursue his enquiries, so he left the path and went over towards the man he had seen.

He went in his own leisurely way, halting frequently to look at some inscription or to examine some piece of able or execrable carving. It was thus that another person, who had entered the grounds some little time after him, was enabled to arrive at the same destination before him.

This was a younger man, one who had numbered considerably less than the tale of years that had been placed to Mr. Herbertson's account. He was thick-set and heavy, but he was dressed as a gentleman, and he moved with a certain air of assurance. He went direct to the attendant and addressed him.

Mr. Herbertson stopped when he saw that he was forestalled, and turned to examine a gorgeous monument which had lately been erected to the memory of an alderman of the City of London. He was some few yards distant from the others, and they did not heed him. Obviously he was no concern of theirs. But in the stillness of the place every word came to him clearly.

"Well," said the new-comer, abruptly. "Any news to-day?"

Mr. Herbertson gave a perceptible start. Still standing before the glory of the departed alderman, he yet turned slightly so that he might get a view of the speaker's face. And when he saw the face he had time to consider it, for the man with the scythe did not answer the question at once. He paused to take a comfortable leaning position upon the shaft of his implement.

It was the accent of the speaker that had first startled Mr. Herbertson, and now he saw that his hearing had not played him false. The young man had a countenance of a peculiar cast. It was not a cast peculiar to a family—a family likeness —but it was suggestive of a foreign type; and if Mr. Herbertson was not mistaken, the face was of a type which he knew well. He waited with keen interest, looking intently at the name of the dead alderman.

"They've been here, sir," said the man with the scythe, "and they haven't gone half-an-hour. You might almost have met them at the gate. They were over there for quite a time. I got talkin' to them, and—and it's all right."

"You got what I wanted?" cried the young man.

"I did, sir. They live at No. 19 Franklyn Crescent, and it's not ten minutes' walk from the gates."

"Ah!" said the visitor; "No. 19 Franklyn Crescent. Ten minutes from the gates."

He uttered the words slowly, as though to impress them upon his memory; and Mr. Herbertson, still intent, noticed something more in his speech than the peculiar accent which had first attracted his attention. It was a note of malevolence, so distinct as to be unmistakable. And Mr. Herbertson, who was a creature of whims and moods, took a dislike to this person who was not sufficiently cultured to keep his baser emotions from the public view. Crude, very!

"That was what you wanted to know, sir—wasn't it?" asked the attendant suggestively.

"Thank you, yes," answered the other. "That was what I wanted to know."

Something passed silently from one to the other. The attendant touched his cap.

"Thank you, sir," he said. "Good mornin', sir."

The young man did not return the "Good morning" by as much as a careless nod. This creature had served his purpose and, having been paid for his service, had no further call upon his attention, no claim upon his civility. He turned to make his way back to the path.

He was thus obliged to pass Mr. Herbertson, who took this opportunity of obtaining a better view of his features. It was apparently a casual glance that passed between them; and what the young man saw was an inconspicuous, middle-aged person, with quiet, reflective eyes, a decidedly informal style of dress and the closely trimmed beard often affected by artists and less commonly by writers. What Mr. Herbertson saw was what he had expected to see, after what he had already seen and heard: the heavy, sombre face of a very strongly built young man, with triumph distinct in it—a triumph that appeared to emphasise the unpleasant characteristics which had been there before.

"The World, the Flesh, and the Devil,—the Tartar devil, too," he reflected, giving a last glance to the tombstone of the departed alderman, whose name he had not even observed. "The World, the Flesh, and the Devil—and especially the two last! Now, I wonder why he is following up those women? It may be a love affair, but his face did not look much like love. Malice and vindictiveness, perhaps, and possibly something worse—but not love. Oh, no, not love!"

He was considerably disturbed—startled, indeed, quite out of his usual easy unconcern. Yet even now his musings were tinged by that humour which was so characteristic of him.

"No," he said, "it did not look much like love. And yet who knows? I may have gleaned an entirely false impression. It is possible that even such a fellow as that might appeal to such a girl as the one I saw.

"Things base and vile, holding no quantity,
Love can transpose to form and dignity."

Upon my word, that quotation has come in after all! Not for me, perhaps, but for the Day. . . . But the strangest part of the whole business is the fact that the girl seemed to have features of the Lusian type, while the man almost certainly spoke with a Lusian accent. I could have sworn to it. Most extraordinary!"

It was some little while before he was able to throw off his unaccustomed soberness and return to the matter of his own business, but he succeeded at last. "Things seem to be happening to-day," he thought. "I seem to have had a glimpse of a melodrama—Act Two, Scene One. But, after all, it can be nothing to me. If the Prince were alive—well, if the Prince were alive he might be interested. These people might quite possibly be fellow countryfolk of his. But he is dead, and I have come here to look at his grave."

With that he moved on to where the attendant was still leaning upon his scythe, watching the departing figure of his late interviewer. He turned to examine Mr. Herbertson with resentment and disgust in his look.

"Good morning," said Mr. Herbertson pleasantly.

"Mornin', sir," answered the man briefly.

The contact was sufficient to restore almost completely Mr. Herbertson's subtle humour. Under its influence he was impelled to play with his subject for a moment or two.

"Do you happen to know," said he, "whether there are any princes buried about here?"

He put the question with a smile, as if it contained an element of the ridiculous. The man's disgust vanished, and he gaped in utter surprise; then, observing the smile, he naturally scented a jest. Possibly he also scented another gratuity.

"Not much," he said. "Not the kind of place for princes."

"Not even foreign princes?" queried Mr. Herbertson. "It was a foreign prince that I was thinking of."

Those playful words proved to be of importance. A new interest awoke in the man questioned, and he looked at the questioner more observingly. But Mr. Herbertson was obviously not a foreigner.

"No," he said. "I don't know of any foreign princes here. But no doubt we get some of the foreign nobility now and again, when they're down and out. And when it comes to that, p'raps one place is as good as another."

"That's true," agreed Mr. Herbertson. "Anyway I suppose they've never complained?"

"Not as I've heard of. . . . Well, there was one of that sort brought here a couple of months back, and his wife and daughter have been coming here ever since. They was here a little bit ago. And if they don't belong to some Upper Ten, I'll eat all this grass!"

The man was surly superficially, but with the loquacity of his type when his interest was awakened. It was not Mr. Herbertson who had awakened his interest, but the ladies in mourning; and it was Mr. Herbertson's lot to get the benefit of some fount of humanity which their plight had unsealed. He got more, for now the man proceeded to relieve himself of a vague uneasiness as well.

"And there's that other gent," he said, "the one that's just gone. He's as good class as them, I should say, though without the taking manner. He's been looking for that family, and only traced them at last by the name over the grave. A friend of theirs he says he is."

There was a pause. In his next words Mr. Herbertson was incautious. He was influenced not only by the suggestion in the man's words but by previous impressions of his own.

"Indeed?" he said. "And have you any reason to doubt it?"

But the question was a mistake. The man stiffened, and took the defensive. There was even a little resentment in his reply.

"Why should I doubt it?" he said curtly. "If he wasn't a friend, why should he be lookin' for them? An' the name's plain enough for anyone to see, friend or not."

"Of course," said Mr. Herbertson, quickly. And then, to ease a situation which had become a little uncomfortable: "It's one of those crosses over there, I suppose?"

"Fourth from the end of the third row. Painted in white letters."

He had evidently finished with the subject, for he turned his eyes to his scythe. Mr. Herbertson spent a moment in consideration. He had only recently decided that this affair was none of his business, but the additional circumstances had naturally aroused his curiosity. Besides, he was offered a simple method of closing the interview.

"Thank you," he said. "I'll go over. Good morning."

"Mornin', sir."

Mr. Herbertson moved away in the direction which had been indicated. He was certainly a little curious. It had occurred to him that he might now discover the name of the young woman whose face had pleased him so well.

Once in that short walk, however, he paused, remembering a previous resolution; quite distinctly a voice spoke to him, the voice whose advice he consistently ignored. "You are a futile person, James," it said; and he knew that now, as always, it said the truth. But now, as always, he went on, and in a few minutes reached the spot which the attendant had pointed out to him.

There he saw one mound which had a small

wooden cross at its head, either as a merely temporary erection or as the modest effort of poverty. He approached it from the back, and was obliged to walk around to the other side before he could see the inscription.

As the man had said, it was lettered in white paint. It took him but an instant to read it, for there was nothing but the name to read:

MATHIAS HAMAR.

Chapter IV

Mr. Herbertson as a Herald of Hope

NUMBER Nineteen Franklyn Crescent was a private house of a comfortable but very inconspicuous appearance. It had forty replicas within three minutes' walk, and perhaps four thousand within a reasonable radius. Mr. Herbertson regarded it with dismay, for it confirmed the fears he had entertained since he had suffered the shock of seeing that name in the cemetery. That cross for Mathias Hamar—and his women here! Disaster could not have been written in plainer terms.

He passed the house, but presently turned back. The shock he had received had awakened all his intuitions, never a negligible quantity in his life, and he was acutely apprehensive. He argued that this might be unreasonable, but ultimately had to defy the warning that would not be silenced. "I need only know," he assured himself. "I need not go further. But I must know. I must know at once, and there is no other way of learning."

The bell was answered by a neatly-dressed elderly woman, definitely English and harmless. "I am looking for a lady of the name of Hamar," said Mr. Herbertson, who had naturally rehearsed the enquiry. "Is she in?"

The woman hesitated in surprise which deepened

to doubt: but a close scrutiny seemed to give her a favourable impression, and she committed herself. "Will you step in?" she said. "I do not know. I will ask."

She closed the door and gave him a chair in the narrow hall. "Please say that I am a friend," said Mr. Herbertson, as he sat down. "Be sure to use the word friend." And distinctly reassured, perhaps by the manner as much as by the words, she nodded, and passed down the hall behind the curtains which shielded the rest of the house. He heard her knock at a door, and he wiped the sweat from his brows. Then there was a low murmur of voices.

The issue was not unexpected. A quicker, lighter footstep sounded in the passage, and a girl came out through the curtains. As he rose she stood for a moment looking at him, with hope and expectation clear in her face; but when she saw a complete stranger, surprise took the place of hope. There was vague recognition from the casual meeting earlier in the morning; but it was not confident recognition.

Mr. Herbertson's doubts, all his intuitions of peril, were being forgotten. It was strange that a glimpse of beauty should have this effect, but it was true.

"Good morning," he said courteously.

"Good morning," said the girl, a little doubtfully and with a slight foreign accent which he recognised with a definite thrill. "But I thought—I thought you said a friend?"

Mr. Herbertson smiled. "Yes," he said. "A friend in a sense, though unknown to you. Let me explain. In the cemetery half an hour ago I saw the name of Hamar on a cross. Years ago, when I visited Styria, I knew a person of that name. Seeing it here so unexpectedly I made enquiries, and the enquiries have brought me to this house."

He spoke slowly, so that she might comprehend: but she was quick of comprehension, and suddenly her face lit up. It was not hope or expectation now, but something akin to joy. Seeing it Mr. Herbertson, always too sensitive to impressions, was convinced of the wisdom of his coming! She dropped the curtains behind her.

"Oh," she cried eagerly. "You knew my father —you knew my father?"

"If your father was the Count Mathias Hamar, of Cronia in Lusia, it is true that I knew him," replied Mr. Herbertson, guardedly but quite cordially.

"And you were friends—you were friends?"

"The Count treated me as a friend," he explained, "and it is quite possible that he might have remembered me if he had met me in England. More I cannot claim."

This speech was a little more difficult, but she put the difficulty aside in favour of the speaker. "Oh, this is a surprise," she cried, "a great surprise. I must take you to my mother. Please come with me."

She held the curtains apart. With a bow he passed through, and she led him down the passage to a closed door. By this time his intuitions had ceased to warn him, and he could not guess that this was the first of a series of interviews which would grow more and more charged with terror as they came to their culmination. Had he known he must surely have turned back from that door and fled the house. Instead, he passed in.

It was a plainly-furnished back-sitting-room, with a pleasant bay window looking into a small but not unlovely garden. There was a low fire in the grate, and in a chair between the window and the fire sat the elderly lady whom he had met with her daughter scarcely an hour ago. She was a lady obviously, with a dignity which would have distinguished her anywhere, but with a kindly and gracious face. Not even the deep stamp of pain and grief, the fragility that spoke of physical weakness, could mask that grace and dignity. She too looked up with swift expectation as the door opened, but the transition to surprise was not so noticeable. Her consideration for the stranger was natural and instinctive.

"Pardon me," murmured the girl, as she brought forward a chair, "I will explain in our own language. It will be better." In a few quick sentences, which Mr. Herbertson followed with equal understanding and appreciation, she made the position clear. He stood until she had finished, and was moved to see the pleasure which lit those troubled eyes, the flush that warmed those sunken cheeks, when the story was told.

"A friend?" said the Countess, in English, "a friend? Then this is the first friend since we came to England!"

She looked at her daughter. Mr. Herbertson bowed. "I am sorry to be only the first," he said. "But I am glad that you receive me as a friend. It was exactly what I hoped."

He sat down, taking his place in the group with

an assurance hardly to be expected in the retiring citizen of Arran Terrace. For a moment there was a pause, while they waited in anxious expectation and hope. Then he gave a further explanation.

"I felt that I must call," he said. "It seemed possible that I might be of service to strangers in a strange land. It is just an enquiry, and if it is not necessary, surely no harm is done. I am an Englishman living now in an English country town; but I lived once in Styria, acting as secretary to a Styrian nobleman. My name is James Herbertson."

The name touched no chord of memory at the time. Mother and daughter looked at one another, and it was the mother that spoke:

"Thank you, Mr. Herbertson. Since you have lived in Styria our story will not seem so incredible to you as it would to most Englishmen. Have you known much lately of Styrian and Lusian affairs?"

"No," said Mr. Herbertson. "I have not kept in touch. My life is a quiet and retired one. But I was greatly surprised to find the name where I did find it."

The Countess bowed her head for a moment. In that moment the room seemed to become charged with tragedy. "Mr. Herbertson," she said then, in a low tone and with quivering lips: "Your surprise was natural. Six months ago we were wealthy and envied, happy and apparently secure at Cronia. Now we have lost all, and my husband is dead."

No words could have made a fitting comment at that point, and the listener did not attempt one. That tragic silence reigned for a long moment, and then the Countess went on:

"You know sufficient to understand a story briefly

told. . . . An enemy has denounced my husband as a Revolutionary. . . . Actually he had taken no part in political movements for many years, but he had failed to remove his name from the roll of a certain Revolutionary Society. This neglect proved fatal, for it gave our foe his opportunity."

The story was told brokenly and lamely, with emotion restrained but inevitable. Mr. Herbertson's sympathy and distress were reflected in his face. After a long pause the gentle voice continued:

"At a few hours' warning we had to leave all and fly. We came to London, where my husband, anxious for concealment, found us this refuge. But he was not a strong man, and the shock of the disaster was aggravated by keen distress of mind. He fell ill, and we could not save him. A few weeks ago he died, leaving us alone."

Again the voice faltered and broke, but there was more distress in Mr. Herbertson's face than in the speaker's. Hers was pain with a noble fortitude, grief borne with a patient dignity. He saw that the girl was watching her mother anxiously and intently, and suddenly realised the significance of her gaze. There was a tragedy in the past, but she dreaded another in the future.

"And you, Mr. Herbertson," added the Countess in a hushed tone, "you are the first to visit us claiming the name of friend. Yours is the first voice to speak to us in England of our home and our happy past. What but a pitying Providence could have sent you?"

Mr. Herbertson sat very still. His features did not betray any welcome of that favouring suggestion. As for the women, they saw only his shocked

and sympathetic face, and could not know that his
warning voices had returned in full chorus, shout-
ing in his quaking heart that he must fly, fly, fly.
He could not fly now, but he knew that he must
take the first opportunity; and as soon as he had
made that wise resolve he abandoned it.

"Yes, Mr. Herbertson," said the girl, warmly.
"Be sure that we shall always be grateful to you
for this kindness—always!"

Mr. Herbertson appeared to recover his self-pos-
session, but with a distinct effort. "I need hardly
say that I am shocked and grieved," he faltered.
"I am more grieved than I can say. But I should
be little of a friend if I said no more than that,
or sought to know no more. Who was this enemy, and why did he betray your husband?"

The Countess looked at her daughter. Mr.
Herbertson looked too, and saw that the girl had
flushed hotly. But she met his look with a faint
smile as her mother replied:

"Our enemy, we are very certain, was a neighbour, who had a son. This son desired our daughter, but Rhona had no desire for him. If you knew
him you would understand. Her refusal, however,
was fatal. They had discovered my husband's secret, and now they threatened him with it. He was
passionate in his indignation, and ordered them from
the house; but within a few days he learned from a
confidential source that a charge had been lodged
against him. It was important that he should remain at liberty, so that he might plead and act, so
he came away before the blow could fall. We pre-
ferred to accompany my husband, and he thought
Rhona would be safer with him. If the Brodes

could do what they had done, they would do anything."

"The Brodes?" murmured Mr. Herbertson.

"Yes. That is the name. Do you know it? Count Brode is one of the chief Lusian loyalists, and an official of the Court and Government."

Mr. Herbertson answered with difficulty. A sudden hoarseness had touched his voice.

"I—I have heard the name. I see it sometimes in the Press news from Styria. But I have another question. Why did you conceal yourselves here? The Count was in no personal danger in England?"

The Countess smiled sadly. "Ah, you do not know the enemy so well as we," she replied. "There are many means ready when the foe is without scruple and high in place, and my husband did not feel safe for a moment. He thought this was best, not only for his own safety, but to give him freedom to act. But here, in exile, his death has left us alone and defenceless."

Mr. Herbertson considered, while pity and wonder mingled in his mind. The action was characteristic of the impulsive and apprehensive Hamar, but it was possible, nevertheless, that he had had good reason for it. Things were different in Lusia and among the Lusians,—and with such an enemy.

"It is very terrible," he said. "The loss and the change. I dare not try to speak of it to you. Believe me, I am able to understand it.—But I wish to speak of another matter. Another person from Lusia is seeking you, and now knows where to find you. Can this be one of your enemies?"

The Countess paled, and the girl sat in startled attention. Quickly Mr. Herbertson described the young man he had seen, every detail of his description finding a signal of response in the faces of his listeners. And when he had told all—

"Yes," said the Countess. "It is indeed one of our enemies. It is Philip Brode!"

Mr. Herbertson was disturbed by the reception of his tidings. "Still," he said, "this young man cannot harm you in England. You need not even see him unless you are willing to do so."

He stopped suddenly at a look from the girl, a look so full of fear and pain that it startled him. "Oh," she cried. "You do not understand—how can you understand? Consider what those men have done! Their presence would kill my mother. If they have found us we must seek some other refuge!"

Mr. Herbertson did consider and did understand. The girl's dread was fully justified, as a swift glance told him. The mother was suddenly downcast and broken, grief and fear having forced the guard of courage and dignity with which she had greeted the visitor. She looked at her daughter with unutterable things in the look, so that the man's heart was stirred to its depths. At last he realised fully "what those men had done." Perhaps they were the only men in Europe who could have done such a deed as this. And the girl answered the mother's look.

"Do not fear, mother," she cried passionately, kneeling at her side and clasping the frail form in protecting arms. "They shall not see you—they shall not reach you! Remember, we have found a friend, and an hour ago we had not one. Oh, they shall never come here—they shall never come here !"

The cry was an appeal as well as a declaration, searching enough to over-ride all considerations save those of pity and mercy. And the broken woman added one more word.

"It was a great folly, that poor little cross. But we could not bear the awful heartlessness of that nameless grave !"

There was another long and painful silence. This interview was full of silences, all of them painful, but those last words had given a deeper horror to the story. Mr. Herbertson was looking past the drooping woman to the garden, but he did not see the garden. He saw a large, lighted room which might have been a room in one of the great houses of a foreign capital. Two men sat at a table with wine before them, and a third stood near, watching them. It was the night when Hamar had given his adhesion to the Thousand through the influence of the eager young fool who had exercised such a fascination over him. They filled their glasses and raised them. "To the Death !" said one, and the other answered "To the Death !" It was the old watchword and pledge of the Thousand. How lightly they had plunged into that Saronio conspiracy, blind to its gravity and its magnitude, blind to its tragic implications, blind to its shame. Here was a little of its aftermath. Oh, how lightly they had talked of death and challenged it! Now they lay together in the Field of the Dead within a stone's throw of one another, and poor Hamar's cross looked over the mounds to find the resting-place of the man who had brought him there. And

his women—Hamar's women—were here. Yes,
they were here, and he, Herbertson, had found
them. He might plead that the Prince was dead,
and that he could do nothing; but the women were
here, destitute and despairing and full of fear. He
might protest that the fear was unnecessary, but it
was useless to reason. They were here.

Those thoughts took but a minute of that long
pause, but they left him helpless. Then he saw
that he was looking out into that suburban garden
which was not unlovely, but far less lovely than his
own. It was far less safe, too, for his own was in
Waldington, forty miles away, in a quiet road where
there was no thoroughfare. His own house? Oh,
that was impossible, of course, but there was that
other house, on the farther side of the brown stone
wall: and Hadfield, stolid, boyish and hearty, and
his bright and kindly little wife. . . .

It took another moment to realise this proposal,
and when it was realised all his intuitions surged
up to forbid it. It was madness, they said, and he
knew that they said truly. But there was the
crushed woman before him, and that lovely girl.
Had the loveliness of the girl much to do with his
decision? He saw that it had not, for if the mother
had been alone the necessity would have been more
urgent, while the danger, surely, would have been
less! No, they were Hamar's women, destitute
and despairing.

Then he was speaking, in reply to that pitiable
excuse for the betraying cross. "I understand
perfectly," he said quite composedly, and with his
hoarseness gone. "It was natural and it was right.
It may prove to have been fortunate, too, for if it

has led an enemy to your door it has also led a friend. And now, Countess, let me beg that you hear me patiently. For I have a plan."

Yes, he had a plan, and he proceeded to give it; and if he risked much in proposing it he certainly had some reward in the joy and relief with which it was received. To those women it meant everything, and they did not seek to conceal the fact. Why, indeed, should they conceal it? And when the first joy and surprise had passed—

"Then it is settled," he said, with decision that was most comforting to hearts without a plan and almost without a hope. "Even if he comes you can keep him at bay for a time. Instruct the woman of the house—let her be prepared. She can use the threat of the police, if necessary. And to-morrow your isolation will be ended."

Yes, he did it well, giving such comfort as may not be measured, and dissipating for the time the black cloud of care which had brooded so long over that lonely couple. Indeed, he did it so well that his coming seemed ever after to be the dawn of a new era, its herald clothed in qualities which he would never have dared to claim. No one knew so well as he how utterly absurd such a claim would have been.

The glory lingered, and he enjoyed it till late in the afternoon. They insisted that he should stay to lunch with them, so that the plan might be perfected, and he was far from unwilling; and as their joy and gratitude warmed him, he proved a very pleasant companion. His memories of Lusia were now ageing, but he had the gift of observation, and had used it well during his stay. Some places

well known to them were also known to him, and
some people: he had actually spoken to the Emperor,
and had met the present Chancellor, Ronnefeldt,
in the days before fame had crowned him. And it
was after they had spoken of Ronnefeldt that he
gave them more of his own story.

It was necessary to do this, though he shrank
from the task. They had refrained from asking
for any personal information which he did not offer,
but it was impossible to withhold it. To-morrow?
No, for it would be more difficult to-morrow.

"Perhaps it is here that I should mention this,"
he said gravely. "The man whom I served in
Styria was a friend of Ronnefeldt's and also a
friend of Count Hamar's. I was reluctant to speak
his name because I know him to have been in some
degree responsible for your present misfortunes. I
refer to the young Prince of Zell, whom I served
in those days as secretary."

How anxiously he waited for the result of the
announcement, how great was his relief when it
proved to be so small! Rhona seemed to have no
definite knowledge of the name, and looked to her
mother for a reply. The Countess was a little
startled, apparently, and tried to remember; but her
recollection was vague and uncertain.

"That unfortunate man?" she said. "You had a
most unhappy master, Mr. Herbertson, and his
name calls up unhappy memories. Yes, my husband and he were friends, but it was before my
marriage. I never met him myself."

There was an awkward silence for a moment:
then, considerate to the utmost, she felt that the
subject should not be pursued, and spoke of some-

thing else. The shadow was past, and Herbert-son wondered at his own trepidation.

When he left, late in the afternoon, it was in an atmosphere of great cordiality; but though the influence of the hour lingered with him for some time after he had left Franklyn Crescent, it did not continue till he reached home. Soon after he left London, indeed, he had lost his confidence as completely as he had lost interest in his evening paper, and the man who stared at the fleeting fields with unseeing and troubled eyes was but a poor shadow of the man who had been a herald of hope to the distressed women from Lusia. For in his heart this man was repeating one word with inexorable conviction and despair.

"Fool, fool, fool!"

Chapter V

Mr. Herbertson Hears the Last Trump

SATURDAY, May the Twentieth, saw the opening of the Second Act of Mr. Herbertson's tragic drama.

The first scene of this Act was as free from evil omen as that chat with the Hadfields over the garden wall. It was tea time, and Mr. Herbertson sat at the head of his table, with the teapot and its satellites before him. He was quite neatly clad, a tribute to his guests and a sign that gardening was over for the day. The table had been generously furnished, the guests having been privileged to choose their favourite pastries and preserves: and there was a home-made cake by Mrs. Jenner, always prepared for these occasions and known to the special circle as "Chum Cake."

The guests were two, Margaret Joan Mead, on Mr. Herbertson's right, facing her friend, Phyllis Barbara Schofield, on his left; but there were two other chairs in which silent guests sat with immovable stolidity, comically unsuspicious of the doom before them. These were "Teddie," a large brown bear, the property of Phyllis, who did not care for dolls, and Princess Mary, the present favourite of Margaret Joan.

These teas were weekly functions, though the guests were not always the same; and they were another problem to the majority of Mr. Herbertson's neighbours. Some, however, remembered with indulgence that most writers were eccentric, while one or two realised a strain of Lewis Carroll or Eugene Field in the man. Probably no one reasoned that the company of children can provide rest and relief for a mind too much troubled with memories. Having no Past themselves, they live in a world whose small talk is unlikely to open up unpleasant topics. Mr. Herbertson's circle, therefore, was well chosen, though the event proved again that there are exceptions to every rule.

The talk began innocently enough. "Margaret is changed to-day, Mr. Herbertson," said Phyllis. "You haven't noticed it yet."

Mr. Herbertson filled the third cup and looked at Margaret. Self-consciousness sat upon her like a garment.

"I can't see any difference," he said consideringly; and Phyllis laughed.

"It's under the table now. It's her new stockings."

Mr. Herbertson looked, and Margaret Joan did not stint her exhibition of the stockings. "But it's not because I'm eight next month," she explained. "It's because of Cousin George. When we were playing in the garden last night he gave me a big push just by the rockery, and my leg is badly scraped. So as I was coming out to tea to-day, and it's Sunday to-morrow, Mamma got the stockings to cover the bandage. They're real silk."

"So if she's grown up it's a sort of accident," said Phyllis Barbara. "She hasn't really reached stocking time."

"Yes. Or else it's Cousin George," said Margaret. "He's a very rough boy, Mr. Herbertson. We hoped he would grow gentler as he growed older, but he doesn't. We have come to the confusion, Mr. Herbertson, that nothing will ever make George a gentle boy."

"Conclusion," suggested her friend.

"It was nearly right," cried Margaret triumphantly. "What does conclusion really mean?"

"The end of anything, or the end of a lot of thinking."

"And so it is. It is the end of our lot of thinking about George."

The operations of tea-taking were little interruption to the talk, though the guests did full justice to the table. "I can't see any good in boys," declared Phyllis Barbara, a brilliant little creature with jet-black bobbed hair and dark eyes of appealing beauty. "They're mostly rough. Haven't I got three brothers, all rough enough for anything? Why, just think—I kissed Cyril one day, and he slapped my face!"

Mr. Herbertson was shocked. "Why *are* boys so rough?" wondered Margaret Joan. "But lots of them must grow out of it somehow. If they didn't, nobody would marry them; and of course we can't do without boys. They grow into fathers."

"And into a few people like Mr. Herbertson," suggested Phyllis, with unexpected politeness. "I wonder if it's the roughest boys that grow into the gentlest men. Were you a very rough boy, Mr. Herbertson?"

"Pretty bad, I'm afraid," answered that gentleman guiltily.

"Then that proves it," said Phyllis Barbara. "What a nice man Cyril will be when he's full grown. I'll let you marry him, Margaret, and then we'll be sisters."

"I'd like to be your sister," was Margaret's answer, after a pause: "and perhaps Cyril will grow up all right. We'll hope for the best. But I don't feel much sub—" she glanced at Mr. Herbertson. "No, I mean *at*-tracted to him. Besides, I'm already engaged."

She made this delicate declaration with a charming blush. Mr. Herbertson met the occasion with an answering blush and a grateful smile. Phyllis Barbara, somewhat piqued, took an unworthy revenge. She glanced at Mr. Herbertson first and then at the well laden table. Probably her life with three rough brothers accounted for occasional maturities and harshnesses in her views and conversation:

"Oh, of course," she said sweetly. "I quite forgot. Well, you're quite right, Margaret, and I hope you'll be scrumptiously happy. But some people know on which side their bread is buttered."

Mr. Herbertson intervened before Margaret could realise the thrust. "I'm sure she'll be scrumptiously happy," he said. "So will the other person. But what are you going to play after tea? I'm sure you have something special in your minds."

The crisis was past. The girls looked at one another with unutterable understanding. Margaret explained:

"That's quite true, Mr. Herbertson. How clever you are to guess. It's a funeral."

"A what?" cried Mr. Herbertson.

"A funeral. We're going to bury Teddy and Princess Mary."

"In your greenhouse, which is going to be Westminster Abbey," added Phyllis Barbara. "And we've brought a Prayer-book, and we're going to share the burying."

"But they're both coming up afterwards," said Margaret Joan. "We've got a trumpet, too—Cyril's trumpet—and we're going to take turns in blowing it, to wake them—like the Last Day, you know. And we do hope you won't mind."

"Oh, he doesn't mind anything," said Phyllis Barbara. "Do you, Mr. Herbertson?"

The pause that followed was slightly prolonged, but ultimately Mr. Herbertson assured them that he did not mind. But he did not pursue what at any other time would have seemed to him a promising topic. He changed the subject.

"And has anything been happening?" he asked. "Within the last few days, I mean."

They considered. "Oh, yes," said Margaret Joan, eagerly. "I remember now. I meant to ask you about it. We had a most exciting talk in our house yesterday. You know my Uncle Albert—George's father? And you know that big earthquake, where thousands of people were killed? Well, Uncle Albert said God did it, to punish them for being wicked."

Her cheeks were warm with indignation. Mr. Herbertson saw the wisdom of treading warily, and held his peace. Not so Phyllis Barbara.

"Well, didn't He?" she asked. "Doesn't He do every mortal thing?"

"Oh, Phyllis!" protested Margaret Joan. "He

couldn't—He just couldn't! There were babies killed in that earthquake, as well as quite innocent animals. He couldn't have done it."

"That does alter the case a bit," admitted Phyllis Barbara. "I suppose the people oughtn't to have gone to live in that earthquaky place. Why, I expect they went there against His will. And then He couldn't be blamed for accidents happening."

"Yes. No doubt they were trespassing. But I didn't mean that. I meant that He wouldn't do such a thing—or perhaps I meant that He couldn't. What *do* I mean, Mr. Herbertson?"

"You mean that because He is good He couldn't do a cruel thing," suggested Mr. Herbertson: and Margaret's face relaxed.

"That's it, exactly," she said. "You always can tell me what I mean." And then with a supreme effort she closed the struggle to express herself.

"He's ever so kinder than people think He is," she said. "So there!"

This time Mr. Herbertson made no attempt to correct the grammar. There was a pause. "We don't talk much about Him in our house," said Phyllis Barbara, taking a further slice of Chum Cake. "But daddy always calls Him 'Good God' when he mentions Him at all. So I guess you're right, Margaret."

Entirely comforted, Margaret Joan turned to finish her tea, while Mr. Herbertson resolved, vaguely, to make notes of the discussion for some future essay. . . . Three or four minutes later he was escorting the two maidens and their dumb friends through his study to the garden.

"All that you see is yours," he said generously. "Presently I will join you. But when do your ladyships go home?"

"Seeing that it's bath-night, we must not be later than seven," replied Margaret Joan.

"We will make a note of it."

He watched them till they had vanished into the fastnesses about his greenhouse, a frequent playground of theirs, inexhaustible in its interest. For the time they were safe and satisfied, and he turned to his study, his easy chair and a cigarette. Before he sat down, however, he remembered an intention, and took from a drawer in his desk a small note-book in which he was accustomed to jot down vagrant suggestions for essays and articles—a gleaner's wallet half filled with neatly entered memoranda. He sat down, lit his cigarette, took out a pencil, and prepared to marshal his notes at leisure.

At leisure, perhaps, but not at ease. He had called the children in to-day to give him that rest and relief which he usually found in their company, but the charm had failed. That chatter about funerals, for instance, so sensitive were his feelings at this time, had thrown him back suddenly into the horrors of the Second of May. And the Last Trump—what a mocking echo of his thoughts as he had entered the cemetery at Maywood Park! For once those charming little friends of his had been cruel, had touched a raw wound with their artless words. And that talk about God—if they had been coached by some arch-tormentor they could not have spoken more aptly to his shrinking conscience.

He opened the book and looked at the last entry with narrowed eyes and furrowed brows. At some tense moment since the Second of May it had flashed into his consciousness from the hinterland of memory, and in some mood of ironic defiance he had set it here. But he had not done so because he feared to forget it or in the prospect of ever writing upon it. Since it had come it had been the last whisper of his conscience every night and the first thought at dawn.

The Mills of God.

He stared at the line till the characters were blurred: then he raised his head and looked down the garden. Faintly from the distance came the voices of the children, who knew nothing of the Mills of God and had not dreamed of wounding him. His face lightening a little, he made another entry:

Ever so Kinder.

The result pleased him. The juxtaposition was so curious. "A contradiction," he mused. "It might be called a New Theology against the Old. How pleasant it would be if Margaret Joan were right, and God never made vengeful earthquakes! But New Theologies are always suspect, perhaps because we know we don't deserve them."

He felt that he could speak for himself at least. With that humble conclusion he laid the book down, knowing that he would never write on that topic and feeling little inclined to make new entries. Indeed, he had scarcely written a line of any kind since the Third of May, for on that day, when the exiles from Styria had "settled in" next door, his peace had gone.

How could it be otherwise? The *cul de sac* of Arran Terrace had suddenly become a thoroughfare in which Pain and Tragedy and Cruelty and Fear trod upon each other's heels. Now Tragedy and Pain had taken rooms in Hadfield's house, and Fear had come to live with him. He could not write, he could scarcely give attention to his beloved garden. Even his favourite books were losing their power of consolation, and there were times when his refuge seemed to have become a prison. . . . And now daily, almost hourly, came the suggestion of flight, a cunning, cowardly, but insistent suggestion. Flight—the last resource, the last infamy.

It was when this suggestion came that he tried to check the drift by calm and ordered reasoning. There lay the abyss. It might be inevitable, but not yet—no, not yet. He shuddered, and shrank back from the verge. So he marshalled his arguments now, finding comfort in the very effort to do so. When he had done so he saw, as he always did, that things were not so bad after all.

On his return on the Second of May he had taken the Hadfields into his confidence to a large extent, and had enlisted their enthusiastic help. It would have been impossible to find a couple more suitable for the task he had offered them. They had declared it to be a privilege, and they were still of the same opinion.

On the next day he had returned to London,
as arranged, and had removed the exiles from
Franklyn Crescent. With the connivance of a
well-rewarded landlady, they had escaped through
a back garden to a waiting car in another street.
Mr. Herbertson had taken no risks, though he
could not understand why the Brodes should
still be so keenly interested in their victims.

In the evening he had brought his new friends
safely to Arran Terrace, where they had found
Marjorie Hadfield awaiting them with a warm-
hearted welcome. When the door had closed
behind them it had shut out a whole world of
disaster, and had given them once more the price-
less gift of a home. In that shelter they had
remained, obviously secure and served by unremitting kindness.

There had been no change in the situation since.
The Countess had been confined to her bed, but a
clever young doctor was in attendance and he had
reported that there was no serious danger. Shock
and strain had brought about a collapse, and the
rest and care now available were the best rem-
edies. Mr. Herbertson had seen neither mother
nor daughter since that first day. There were
good reasons why he should not try to see them,
and as a matter of fact he had no wish to do so.
He had done enough. Life in Arran Terrace, so
rudely disturbed, must now flow on almost as
before!

"Well, it's not so bad," he thought, looking upon
his work and finding that it was good. "When one
looks at things calmly there is really no need for

apprehension. I am very foolish—I am actually becoming morbid. I must get back to work again, and to my books, and let the future look after itself. I must see more of those children—even if they do play funeral games! . . . Tut! tut! The Last Trump, indeed!"

Considerably calmed, and with resolution in his face, he rose and went to his crowded bookcase. He could not return to his gardening just now, but half an hour of the atmosphere of Alexander Smith's *Dreamthorp* would surely complete the cure of his morbidity. He found the book and returned to his chair.

The book opened with the ease of frequent use, but just as he reached a favourite essay he was brought to a pause. There was a short, sharp ring at the doorbell of his house. Then came another sound, this from the bottom of the garden. It was the bleat of a toy trumpet. The children had reached the stage of the Last Trump, and were blowing to wake the dead.

Mr. Herbertson smiled as he realised and remembered. He was so far restored now that he despised himself for having linked that toy trumpet with his own curious reflection on entering Maywood Park Cemetery on the Second of May. He could not dream that in the coincidence of the doorbell and the trumpet a sardonic Destiny might be mingling mockery with menace.

Chapter VI

Mr. Herbertson Affords Certain Glimpses of the Past

HE heard Mrs. Jenner go to the front door and open it. He heard a man's voice, and the door was closed. Mrs. Jenner came to the study.

"It is Dr. Henslow, sir. He would like to see you for a moment."

"Indeed?" said Mr. Herbertson, a little surprised but all unsuspicious. "Oh, bring him in here."

He rose as the doctor's tread approached the threshold. Henslow was a young man whose high qualifications and real ability, advantaged by a frank, engaging manner, had won him a good position in the neighbourhood within the last twelve months. He had never had occasion to visit Mr. Herbertson before, and he came now as a stranger. But Mr. Herbertson had known him by repute, had seen him, and had liked him. The fellow was so pleasingly unprofessional, with his gray tweeds, his keen, dark features, and the eyes whose glance had so much friendliness in its directness.

"Please come in," he said. "Take that chair. Will you have a cigarette—or a cigar?"

"Not just now, if you please," said Henslow. "I have to make a call a few doors away."

As he spoke and sat down he was taking impressions, and they were all favourable. This very comfortable room, with its maximum of good books, its minimum of pictures, also good, its large and serviceable writing table and its clear outlook to a luxuriant garden—all these were quite to his taste. This urbane and evidently cultured man of middle age was quite to his taste too, and he was immediately at his ease.

"Thanks all the same," he added quickly. "But do I interrupt your reading?"

"Not at all," said Mr. Herbertson. "I had just opened Alexander Smith, but we hadn't actually spoken to each other."

"Then you know an old acquaintance of mine," said the doctor, with the friendliness a bookman always feels for a kindred spirit newly discovered. "He is a good companion for a sunny afternoon. But that pleasant world of his does not bear inspection, I am afraid. He is quite frank about it when he calls it Dreamthorp."

Mr. Herbertson seemed to examine that criticism. At least he did not hasten to reply. His silence was a check, and Henslow, quick in his perceptions, fancied that he might have been too precipitate. This excellent room, with its happily arranged garden outlook—and the man was a writer, was he not? Well, it would be quite easy for some men to build a Dreamthorp in Arran Terrace.

"But it is a very good world to get away to for a rest," he added. "Happy illusion may be a useful refuge. I see that we must have a talk about Alexander Smith another day—if you can spare me the time. To-day I have called about my patient next door—Mrs. Franks."

Mr. Herbertson returned from Dreamthorp with a slight shadow upon his urbanity; but he was not yet apprehensive.

"Yes?" he said.

"I understand that this lady is a friend of yours?"

Mr. Herbertson waited a moment, but not even a keen observer could have guessed how his every instinct had sprung to arms.

"That is so," he answered, quite normally, after a pause.

"I asked Mrs. Hadfield," proceeded the doctor, "and she suggested that I should consult you. The fact is that I am in a difficulty with regard to my patient. Up to a certain point she made normal and quite satisfactory progress. I could not have expected anything better. But that has ceased, and for several days there have been rather disquieting symptoms. Well, to put it plainly, there is a definite hindrance to her recovery, and unless it is removed . . ."

He paused.

"This sounds serious," said Mr. Herbertson, his own alarm having abated for the moment.

"It threatens to become serious. That is why I come to you. You may be able to do more—as a friend—than I can do as a physician. I have no medicine for a mind diseased, but you may know of something that will help."

"You refer to her grief and sense of loss?"

"No. Those are present, but there is also something else. There is—fear."

"Fear?"

"Yes, fear. There is an apprehension which appears to become more and more acute as time passes. I cannot remove it—you see, I do not know the circumstances. The daughter does know, but she has failed to remove it. So as you had called me in to this case, I felt that I must report the position to you."

Mr. Herbertson sat very still. It was clear that he was impressed, and Henslow was satisfied that he had produced the right impression. But Mr. Herbertson was more than impressed. All his alarm had returned with strong reinforcements. He tried to hold his own—to maintain the attitude of the friend who is considerably interested and becomes concerned upon the receipt of an unfavourable report. He succeeded quite well, but Henslow had a curious feeling from that point up to the end of the conversation. It was the feeling that this man was somehow on the defensive, that he was arguing against his own convictions.

Fear!

"This is indeed serious," said Mr. Herbertson gravely. "Yet I suppose it was only to be expected. Of course you know some of the circumstances, if not all. They are nothing less than tragic. These people have not only lost all their means within a few months, but they have been bereaved by the death of the husband and father."

The doctor nodded. "I am aware of the presence of a great sorrow," he said, "but that is not the trouble. That is in the past. Fear is an active element of the present—or the future. My patient is suffering from what seems to be a haunting dread of some impending evil—a dread which actually deepens as her strength returns. I am not sure whether it is on her own or her daughter's behalf—perhaps the daughter's chiefly. But unless something can be done to calm her, to dissipate the—well, the fear—she will make no progress."

Still Mr. Herbertson used reason, grave and assured. "Trouble always breeds dread," he said. "One who has been struck usually expects, or fears, another blow. Is it anything more than that?"

"I am afraid it is."

Henslow's expression said more than his words. There was a long pause before Mr. Herbertson spoke again, and then he seemed to have been convinced.

"Well, I am sorry to hear it," he said. "Of course I will do what I can at once. I will give her assurances which will relieve her mind if any assurances can do so."

Dr. Henslow rose. "Thank you," he said heartily. "That may help us. I felt that my best course was to explain my difficulty to you. I trust that you will not consider me too careful or too officious?"

"No—indeed no. I am very glad that you have spoken."

He could not have said more, and his manner was sufficiently cordial as he escorted his visitor to the door and said good-bye. At the time the young doctor was quite satisfied, and it was only afterwards that he recalled an earlier impression of the interview. A man on the defensive? Probably a false impression after all.

Mr. Herbertson returned to his study with considerable dissatisfaction. He did not sit down for some time, but stood staring out into a garden which he did not see.

"Fear!" he muttered.

Then he looked around the room. He saw his *Dreamthorp* lying upon a chair, closed it impatiently, and set it back in its place. He treated it almost rudely. Then he saw his notebook upon the writing table, and pushed it hastily back into his drawer. *The Mills of God.* After that he sat down to write, wording his message with great care.

I understand from Dr. Henslow that your mother is suffering from a nervous apprehension of danger. *There is no danger.* Will you try to assure her of this? We are all so anxious to see her quite well.

J. H.

He took this to Mrs. Jenner for delivery. "With my respects, Mrs. Jenner," he said. "And I hope that Mrs. Franks will soon be better."

"Yes, sir," said Mrs. Jenner, glad of the errand. "I will take it at once."

Mr. Herbertson turned away. She did not hear him mutter scornfully: "Words, words, words!" He returned to his study and his chair, and sat there for a considerable time with scarcely a movement. For the present he had abandoned all specifics and surrendered to the weakness and peril of uncontrolled reverie. Between the man and his garden the old ghosts walked, ghastly and appalling.

It was the children who brought relief. Presently a clock struck seven. Then came voices, and footsteps on the crazy path that led from his study to the garden. The ghosts vanished.

"As a chum you're the limit, Mr. Herbertson," said Margaret Joan. "You've left us all to ourselves in your greenhouse all the time. You never even dreamed that we might be getting into mischief."

"You'll always think the best of me, I'm sure," said their host, who had forgotten them entirely; and Margaret seemed a trifle puzzled.

"There isn't anything else to think about you," she said, quite casually; whereupon Mr. Herbertson's soul blushed, if a soul may be said to do such a thing. This world of illusion was a kindly world as long as it lasted!

"We had the funeral all right," said Phyllis Barbara. "The grave—I mean the vault—was the underground of your greenhouse. The only thing was that the buried ones couldn't come up by themselves when we blew the trumpet. We had to go down and get them."

"Well, we can't have everything in a make-believe," said Mr. Herbertson, already calmed by their presence and their comforting innocence. "But now, I suppose, you want me to take you home. —After a course of Swiss Roll?"

They agreed that this was the programme, and it was duly carried out. Ten minutes later he issued from the house with his guests, to leave them at their own doors with the understanding that he would escort them both to morning service at St. Augustine's next day. Then he returned to face his own problems in solitude, a little fortified by that pleasant contact with his appointed protectors.

But their comfort did not last long, and he was in a restless and troubled mood an hour later when Hadfield came in for a chat. Because he was restless and troubled he said more than he had said before, and said it with less than his usual self-control. It was his way of seeking that sympathy and help which no one could supply.

Since the arrival of the strangers Hadfield had quite failed to recover his equilibrium. Under his very ordinary and somewhat stolid exterior bubbled a boyish excitement and exaltation which often found an outlet in conversation with his neighbour because it could not betray itself elsewhere. It seemed to him that his plain and straightforward existence had been transformed, or that he had stepped over its borders into a realm peopled with the mighty. He had a great respect for the mighty, and it was no small thing to find that his next-door neighbour was the one-time secretary to a prince, and a partner in Revolution; it was naturally a still greater thing that he should be sheltering under his own roof a countess and the daughter of a countess. It was as much as he could do to keep the secret, and a hundred times a day he tried to imagine the scene which would follow if he should drop it into the serene atmosphere of his office. So his visits had been frequent during the last three weeks, and Mr. Herbertson appeared to welcome them. They supplied occupation for the quietest hour of the day, when man is prone to unprofitable musings.

"Things going well?" queried Mr. Herbertson, as he produced his cigars.

"At the office? Yes, thanks. But nothing ever happens there, you know."

Probably the business of the Urban District Council had seemed somewhat humdrum during the last week or two. And then his enthusiasm bubbled over.

"I say," he remarked. "I can't help being glad that you brought them to us. I mean the ladies. They're awfully nice people."

"Really?"

"Yes. There's no nonsense about them, you know, and no side. No one would think they were of the nobility."

Mr. Herbertson smiled, perhaps at Hadfield's conception of the manner in which the pride of race and place might have displayed itself. "You're quite right," he agreed. "They have the kind hearts which are more than coronets— But, by the way, I have done my best to assure them that they are both quite safe here—that no one will dare to annoy them. I understand that the Countess is apprehensive. You might mention this to your wife, so that she may use any opportunity of confirming my assurances."

"That's a good idea," said Hadfield emphatically. "I'll see to it. It's that Count Philip, I suppose. For my own part, I should like nothing better than to get him into the house and give him a bit of my mind."

Mr. Herbertson's ironic self tried to picture the meeting! The young man went on:

"The best thing, I suppose, would be good news of some kind. Is there no chance of that—I mean, from their home?"

It was difficult to make Hadfield understand. He was so insular in his thinking and so confined in his life. He was not a reader, and had no sense of history, so that while he was the most docile of pupils he was also the slowest of scholars. During recent days he had done his best with the daily papers, asking questions after reading, and making every effort to remember. He knew of the historic struggle of the Salzburgs to unify an Empire whose component parts seemed no more able to coalesce than oil and water, and he knew how the Saronio Conspiracy of twenty-five years ago had mocked and frustrated the good intentions of the present Emperor. He had also gathered certain impressions of his neighbour's quondam master, Ferdinand's nephew, that egregious Prince of Zell who had first betrayed his sovereign by treachery and had afterwards betrayed his associates by flight: but Herbertson found too often that he had misread what he had read and was nursing a comically perverted impression of the truth. He failed to see any virtue in the ancient feud between Styria and Lusia, but this failure was not due to his common sense. It was due to his lack of imagination, his inability to set himself in another man's place. The ancient Iron Crown of Lusia?—Oh, well enough for a museum, no doubt, but why make a fuss about it any more? Put it in its glass case, and get on with the job!

So it was that he had a vague idea of good news for the Hamars—something in the way of a solicitor's letter enclosing passports and pardons, with dates of sailings. Now Herbertson sighed, smiled, and once more tried to explain, opening out, in the effort, more of his past than he had ever revealed before.

"My dear fellow—" he began. Then he paused, considered, and at last proceeded on a lower key.

"My dear fellow, you don't appreciate the difficulties. This matter does not stand alone—on its own merits. It has its roots in that old Saronio business. Count Hamar was the intimate friend of Adrian of Zell, and went into the plot with him. It is impossible to appeal to the Emperor without re-opening that shameful chapter—a most painful personal chapter. And who would re-open it? There is no man living who would dare to mention Adrian's name in the old man's presence."

"So bad as that?" muttered Hadfield.

"Worse than that. Try to see it as they see it over there—as one of the most infamous things in modern history. That great man—for he is a great man—after many disappointments in his own family, placed the most complete faith and affection in this boy. He was the son of his favourite sister, and he brought him up from Zell to be the darling of the Court. He treated him in such a way that he was called the Apple of the Eagle's Eye. And, after all, the young fool allowed himself to become the centre, the pivot, the figure-head of a plot whose success would have broken the Empire in two. . . . Why, there are no words that can measure the blackness of it!"

Hadfield was impressed now. But his friend had not yet finished.

"But it was even worse than that," he went on. "If the fool had acted decently at the end there would have been something to say for him. He might have faced it out in half a dozen ways, or he might have cut the knot by a simple suicide. But any one of those courses would have needed courage of some kind, and he hadn't any. A coward, Hadfield, and therefore a lost soul when it came to the crisis. And that was the last straw—in Ferdinand's eyes the unpardonable sin. On one point the Salzburg code of honour is inflexible. It can forgive everything but the White Feather. That get-away was the end of Adrian. That other end, when I buried him in Maywood Park, was of no importance to anybody."

Hadfield noticed the strain that had crept into Herbertson's tones. "I suppose nothing can save a coward," he said sympathetically. "He is the hopeless case."

"Quite. Anyway he showed no heart for the right course. It may be that I failed him myself —I was the only person with him at the time—but of course I could not command him. And at any rate I did the next best thing by standing by him till I buried him in that forgotten grave. But those years of wandering with my Coward, Hadfield, are still a nightmare to me!"

"They must be. . . . But, by the way, I never asked you—what did he die of?"

That was the real Hadfield—off at a tangent. There was a longer pause after the question—so long that he began to doubt if his friend had heard. But the answer came.

"There was a formidable medical name for it, old fellow—you shall read it presently, though it won't be of much use to you. But I think I may say, between ourselves, that he had become oppressed by a sense of his own futility, and had no will to live. Indeed, a sentimentalist might declare that he died of a broken heart. For after all, you know, he was not a blockhead, and though he talked little, I know that he realised what he had done —and lost. And now, as we see, his folly works on, though he lies under a forgotten mound where no one has ever placed a flower. The man who never did any good with his life is doing big mischief years after his death. I could wish him nothing worse than that he should see what he has done."

"Come," protested Hadfield, "this is not entirely his work, you know. There are other villains in it."

"His crime is their opportunity. But for him these horrors could not have happened. So his folly carries on through the years, wounding to right and left."

The talk had certainly given Hadfield a clearer view of the situation in Styria, and also a new view of Mr. Herbertson. What a tragedy lay in the hinterland of this man's quiet life! By Jove, who would have guessed it! As for Herbertson, the talk had given him considerable relief, whether Hadfield understood or not.

"So you see how slight is the prospect of good news," he said. "There is no one to re-open the question, and an enemy keeps the gate. We can do nothing. If Hamar had lived an appeal would have been possible, but now. To put it plainly, we cannot expect any news, though of course we must not say so. Despair must not be allowed to reach the bedside. And there is no real cause for fear, so we must keep that out too. The Brodes have got all they want—or, at least, all they can hope to get. They are not likely to follow further."

Even as he spoke he remembered, with sudden discomfort, Philip's expression in the cemetery. "If they call I hope it will be when I am at home," said Hadfield. And Herbertson smiled. He had certainly brought his refugees to the right place! This young man might have little imagination, but he had great loyalty.

"That's the note," he said. "A good kicking would do them a world of good. But in the meantime I'm going to lend you a little book I wrote years ago, soon after I settled here. It will help you to see the situation squarely. And if you feel that I've dealt rather severely with my old master, —he is in Chapter Seven—just look at some of the results of his work. You have them near enough at hand!"

They chatted a little longer, but not on the same topic; then, as darkness was falling, Herbertson went in to find that little book, *The Styrian Riddle,* which he had discussed with Mr. MacArthur on the day of days. Then they parted with a new confidence between them, Herbertson to his study and Hadfield to the chatter of his vivacious little wife and the leisurely reading of his *Riddle,* with special reference to Chapter Seven. That chapter was headed "Adrian of Zell" and it was the story of a pitiful failure, told without pity. He was able, now, to understand the attitude of Mr. Herbertson towards his former master, but he was not quite able to sympathise with it. As he told his wife, too, it was difficult to recognise in the harsh, cynical critic of the preposterous Prince of Zell the man who was such a good neighbour.

"But there," he concluded wisely, full of thought after the talk in the garden and the reading of the story. "One cannot really tell what took place between the two. And anyway most men have quite a store of unsuspected—er—er, characteristics below the surface that they show every day. What do you say, Madge?"

"I hope that all your hidden characteristics are good ones," said Mrs. Hadfield, who had been immersed in problems of bed and board. "Then I may get a pleasant surprise now and then."

Hadfield considered that remark very carefully, but before he had come to a conclusion about it his wife uttered another. She was in a happy and mischievous mood.

"And I am quite sure," she said, "that before Mr. Herbertson has finished with you I shall have a very wise husband. Which was beyond my wildest dreams. . . ."

It was about this time that Mr. Herbertson went to bed, somewhat relieved by his talk with Hadfield and by the confidences he had given. He had recovered poise, and was inclined to blame himself for his previous agitation. He had allowed the merest trifles to alarm him, as though he had been the unfortunate possessor of a guilty conscience. "But that is not the case," he decided, as he turned out his last light. "It is not by any means the case. I have done all that I could do. I have done all that any man could do. . . . And so to bed!"

But some mocking memory spoke out of the dark: "Words, words, words!"

Chapter VII

A Man Breaks Into the Garden

THE Third Scene of the Second Act shows Mr. Herbertson continuing his effort to save his world in Arran Terrace. He continued it with pathetic perseverance but with unsatisfactory results. Events were on the march, and his resistance was of little more avail than Mrs. Partington's broom against the flowing tide.

A restless night was poor preparation for a trying day, but the morning did at least put to flight a legion of ghosts and voices. It did not rid him of the indisputable reality. A tour in his garden after breakfast did him a little good until he chanced to look up at the back windows of Hadfield's house. Behind those windows were the exiles from Styria, and from that moment the garden ceased to be the refuge it had been. It was still his place of retreat, but it was vulnerable. He was glad when he saw that it was time to keep his appointment with the children.

He returned to the house, and it was on returning to the house that he enjoyed the one bright moment of that troubled day. Mrs. Jenner had made her morning inquiry next door, and brought good news. The Countess (known to her, of course, as "Mrs. Franks") had spent a better night.

She had had two or three hours of quiet sleep. Mr. Herbertson went upstairs with a lighter brow.

"The result of my message," he thought. "It has done good already. Excellent!" So ten minutes later, when he went out to meet his friends, he was almost as cheerful a comrade as ever until they reached the church and their chatter was hushed in that atmosphere of solemnity which gave the children so much pleasure.

Mr. Herbertson did not enjoy worship at St. Augustine's. His critical and artistic sense revolted against a service which consisted largely of the unintelligible mouthing of sonorous sentences, the calculated mutilation of the beautiful, crowned too often by a crude schoolboy essay in theology. But the children loved the experience, and he loved their company through the ordeal and their comments afterwards.

To-day, however, the comfort was inadequate because the experience was so unfortunate. The preacher was the newest curate, one whom Mr. Herbertson had dubbed "egregious" at the very first hearing: and this egregious young man had chosen as his text a phrase which expressed a grim old Law—"Without the shedding of blood there is no Remission of Sins." It set Mr. Herbertson thinking of the Code of the Salzburgs, as described to Hadfield yesterday. He did not hear the sermon, in which, no doubt, the old Law was comfortably explained away. . . . In some ways the old Law and the Salzburg Code were identical, and no coward could face either. If Adrian had shot himself, for instance, he would have met the demands of the Code as far as a man might, and a

good many people would have forgiven him. . . .
And from this point Mr. Herbertson was lost in a
maze of profitless musings.   No, they were worse
than profitless, for they left him disturbed, irritated,
quite unable to enjoy the company of his little
friends.   Confound that curate!   Why did they
allow mere boys to meddle with themes so tremendous?   It was like these children yesterday,
playing with the Last Trump. . . . But at last the
curate said "Amen!" and the ordeal was over.

He took the children for their usual walk for
half an hour after church, but he could not recap-
ture the lost charm.   They felt that something
was wrong, and, in the way of children, avoided the
problem of their grown-up friend by turning to topics
of greater interest to themselves—the sleekness of
the egregious curate's hair, for instance, and the
probable amount of the offertory.   When they had
parted in Arran Terrace he realised with a little
shock that the parting had been something of a
relief to him.   A relief!   For the first time!

He went in to his solitary dinner, and over dinner made a stand once more.   "This is absurd,"
he decided.   "It must stop.   It is all imagination
—a morbid imagination. . . . I will take a long
walk this afternoon, and cure my megrims.   Confound that curate!"

He took the walk, but it failed to achieve its
purpose.   Doubtful whether he should invite Hadfield's company or not, he at last decided to go
alone.   Hadfield would certainly return to the topic
which Herbertson wished to avoid, so it was wiser
to go without him.   But no man takes a solitary
walk alone, and Herbertson's inevitable companion

was little of a comforter. He, too, found the topic irresistible, and his references and approaches were artful and insidious. Besides, it was impossible to turn his interest into other channels for more than a minute or so, and when the walk was over the sufferer was sorry that he had left Hadfield behind. He had also realised that since his circle of friends was so small, and his situation so peculiar, it would be very difficult to avoid the topic for any length of time. It had come to dwell in Arran Terrace. It could not go back, for you cannot reverse the Mills. And Arran Terrace was a *cul de sac!*

Nevertheless he maintained the struggle for yet a little longer. His carefully constructed world was not to be given up so lightly. He spent the first two hours after tea in a survey of his garden, with a little light work thrown in; and he spent the remainder among his books, with the low fire of Mrs. Jenner's prudent care to make things cosy, and with his favourites spread out beneath his green-shaded reading lamp. He revived certain impressions of Marcus Aurelius that evening, that wise man who in a world of tremendous realities had insisted that the only world of reality was that which a man made for himself in the citadel of his own soul. After a light supper he read till ten and then laid his books aside with a sense of satisfaction. They had not lost their charm, after all. Or rather, he was recovering it by a resolute effort of will. Yes, that was a better way of putting it. And true!

As a last item on the programme of a troubled day he decided that he would do what he often did—take a final survey of his garden. Quite recently a street of new houses had been built overlooking his grounds at the back, and he had reason to believe that one or two boys from those houses had already visited his premises at night. Passing through the house, therefore, he entered the garden, moving silently along on the turf and carefully avoiding all overhanging branches. But though his eyes and ears were keenly on the alert, his mind was busy with the problem which had been so troublesome through all the past days. It was absolutely impossible to get away from it, even with the help of Marcus Aurelius!

Suddenly he stopped and stood quite still. Had he heard a sound? He waited, peering through a curtain of foliage.

He had just reached the limit of his house-plot, where the brown-stone wall ended that divided his own garden from Hadfield's. Another moment and the sound was repeated, and he felt sure that it came from that wall. He moved forward a little to avoid the screen of branches that hung before him.

It was dark now, but it was a summer darkness; and as things began to shape themselves, he saw that there was indeed a trespasser upon the premises. Some one was actually standing at the wall with his elbows upon it, peering over. It was not a boy, but a man.

Mr. Herbertson was bewildered for a moment, but only for a moment. Hadfield's back rooms were all lit up, and the blinds had not been drawn. The visitor was watching those rooms at his leisure, secure from observation, but with greater advantages than he could have obtained by a call at the front door.

Mr. Herbertson trembled with indignation, not unmingled with something less noble; for he was not by any means a man of war. But after a moment's agitation he moved stealthily forward, and, familiar with every inch of the way, approached to within an arm's length of the spy. And that gentleman was so absorbed in his work that he had eyes for nothing else.

"You blackguard!" said Mr. Herbertson hoarsely.

At the same instant, with the impulsive rage of the man who is unaccustomed to emergencies, he seized the fellow's collar. For a moment they faced each other in a breathless silence, and then the eavesdropper took a natural course. He swung round and under his captor's arm, wrenching his collar free by the movement and sending Mr. Herbertson staggering back across the path. Then he made a gallant effort to escape.

He had entered the garden by means of the farther wall, near which the new street had been built, and it was his intention to go as he had come. The sudden attack, however, had thrown him into confusion, and he had been staring for some time at lighted windows. He plunged straight from the wall into a strawberry bed, caught a glimpse of friendly lights in the distance, and made a bee-line for them. Suddenly an unfinished building loomed before him, and he stumbled over something that lay upon the ground. Another instant, and he found the solid earth slip from beneath him, flung out his arms wildly, and caught a plank that seemed to bridge the chasm. He had slipped into the entrance to that subterranean chamber which Margaret Joan and Phyllis Barbara had utilised as a "vault," and which was being prepared as a winter storehouse for fragile plants when the marvellous new greenhouse should be in full commission. He believed, however, that he was hanging over a well, and was breathless with the shock and with terror. He clutched mightily and swore dreadfully. Immediately Mr. Herbertson came, armed with a stout garden stake.

"My God!" gasped the victim, "give me a hand, will you? I can't hold on another minute!"

"You had better!" said Mr. Herbertson. "What are you doing in my garden?"

It was a cruel question. The man swore again, and then began to raise himself over the plank.

"If you move," said Mr. Herbertson, "I'll knock you over the head."

There was hard breathing for a few seconds. The man saw the club, and considered. Indeed, his first fright was passing.

"Don't do that, sir," he said, with something akin to a whine. "I haven't been doing any harm."

At once the interview dropped to a less heroic plane. Mr. Herbertson lowered his weapon.

"If you move," he said, "I keep my word. Now, tell me what you wanted here, and who sent you."

There was silence. They could see each other now without difficulty. "Speak out, man," said Mr. Herbertson. "Who sent you? If you don't, I'll call my neighbour, and you shall be given in charge."

That was a very reasonable course, and might

have unpleasant consequences. The eavesdropper saw that it would not serve the purposes of his employers.

"Come," he said, "there's no need for that. Only let me up out of this, and I'll tell you all about it."

"You're better where you are," was the firm reply. "And the sooner you speak the sooner you'll be out. Who sent you?"

The prisoner undoubtedly thought unutterable things. But he clutched his plank despairingly, and spoke:

"I'm from Dovetons'."

"Oh. The private enquiry rascals. Go on."

"I've nothing to do with you at all, and I wouldn't have hurt your garden. It's next door I'm looking after. And I only wanted to see some people who are staying there."

"And have you seen them?"

There was another pause, but the man had resolved to be frank.

"I've seen a young lady. That's all.—Good God, I'm falling!"

"Who is your employer?" asked Mr. Herbertson mercilessly. "Quick!"

"I don't know—my oath I don't. I only obey orders."

Mr. Herbertson, of course, could have answered the question himself without difficulty, and he did not linger on this point. Folly was urging him further.

"I want to know one thing," he said. "His address. If you can tell me that, I'll let you go."

There was another brief halt. The fellow saw an opportunity for a lie, but was not quite sure of

its success. He had gained an impression that Mr.
Herbertson knew a good deal.

"I heard an address," he gasped, "one day in
the office. If it's not right, I don't know any other.
It's the Hotel Petersburg."

"Very good. Now you can climb out."

The fellow did so with considerable fluster,
hard breathing, and humiliation, brushed the earth
from his hands, picked up his hat, and peered
curiously at his captor in the darkness. But his
captor had already finished with him, and now
polished him off with uncharacteristic decision.

"I'll show you the way out," he said—"an easier
one than the wall. But if you show your face in
the neighbourhood again you will be sorry for it.
Follow me."

He led the man out by the garden door, and did
not leave him until he was safe on the pavement
of Arran Terrace. And when the fellow had
reached the pavement Mr. Herbertson closed the
gate upon him without a word, a course which filled
the other with uneasy astonishment. But he did
not think it wise to linger. He had achieved his
purpose, and his final misadventure was a thing
which need not be revealed to his employers.

Mr. Herbertson returned to his study. His
peace was gone. He sat down, quivering, throbbing, tremulous in every nerve. What now?

He did not know. It was a considerable time
before he could get his thoughts into any semblance
of order. His assurances of yesterday, his brave
arguments, conclusions and resolves. Words,
Words, Words!

Out of the chaos at last came a question—*Why?*

The destroyers were not satisfied with what they had done. They were tracking their victims from place to place. First Philip's evil face in the cemetery: now the man in the garden. They meant to keep in touch. Why? From that point things began to arrange themselves. He had to bend all the energies of his mind to find the answer, and order followed the effort.

In the search for an answer Mr. Herbertson went as far as Styria. He knew these kinds of men well enough, and he tried to trace the tortuous and hidden outline of their plans. Because he knew them, and because he was not a stupid man, he succeeded at last. The solution flashed out, leaving him hot with rage and indignation.

"The devils!" he muttered.

It was so clear, so convincing, so like the amazingly efficient and far-sighted Brode. . . . Then Mr. Herbertson began to wonder how it was that he had solved the riddle. Had his garden given him something of the wisdom of the serpent?

But what was to be done? Here, however, was a question easier of answer. Nothing could be done. Of course not. There was no one to do it. Things must take their course. Their course . . .

And shortly afterwards Mr. Herbertson rose and went upstairs. . . . No, nothing could be done . . . and the one thing that had suggested itself was utterly impossible.

It was the maddest thought of this mad day.

Chapter VIII

Mr. Herbertson, Some Spectres, and a Goddess

MR. HERBERTSON was in his garden early next morning. He did not even pause in his study to bring up to date the calendar which was not Shakespearean. For the whole morning of that Monday it spoke shamelessly of Sunday, the twenty-first. Its owner had no place for dates, and his harmless habits were in confusion.

He reached the scene of his adventure and looked soberly upon the evidences. He had not dared to hope that it might have been a dream, but there was dismay as well as conviction in this disorder. His one impulse was to repair the damage before any one else should see it and spread the news.

He found some satisfaction in the task. It was obviously the Next Thing, and such a situation is balm to perplexity. It also worked in with his campaign of defence, and that was an agreeable fact. When Mrs. Jenner came out presently with two letters and some good news he had removed all marks, whether of the cloven hoof or of the Mills of God. Moreover, the work and its success had done him good.

"I have enquired about Mrs. Franks, sir," said

the housekeeper. "She has had another good night."

"Glad to hear it," said Mr. Herbertson, almost heartily.

"She slept most of the night, and is quite composed this morning. Ah, there's nothing like sleep."

"No," said Mr. Herbertson. "It knits up the ravelled sleeve of Care. It is also good to have a composed mind; and it is almost impossible to have the one without the other."

"No, indeed," said Mrs. Jenner, cautiously. "But there's something more, sir. Mrs. Hadfield says that the young lady thinks that her mother might be the better for a visit from you."

"From me?" said Mr. Herbertson.

"Yes, sir."

He was taken aback. Mrs. Jenner, however, read his consternation as surprise.

"So she must be getting on nicely," she said. "Still, it can hardly be for a day or two. Of course the Doctor will say when. They are going to ask him."

Mr. Herbertson had had time to recover. After all, this development, however embarrassing, was only natural and inevitable. He had simply been too preoccupied to foresee it.

"Of course," he said. "Of course. Doctor Henslow will settle that. Thank you for your good news—and the letters. And I will come up to breakfast presently with all my heart."

Mrs. Jenner retired to prepare the breakfast, and he sat down on a bench near his greenhouse to open the letters. They were quite good letters, one of them containing a cheque from one of his

Editors—a welcome attention from the world which he was trying to save. . . . Things were not so bad, after all. He had removed all trace of the invasion of his garden, and no one could know. . . . It would be awkward to have to visit the Countess, for he did not love a lie; but the visit might be postponed for some time yet. He need not meet trouble half way.

At twenty minutes to nine he went up towards the house, in time to exchange greetings with Margaret Joan across the intervening gardens. She promised to come in and see him, bringing a kiss or two, after tea, and he promised to welcome her with open arms. Then she fled to join her Phyllis, and Mr. Herbertson went in to his bathroom and his breakfast.

At breakfast he felt so much restored that he could turn without a tremor to the weekly Styrian letter in his *Daily Telegraph*. There he read that the Emperor was resting at his Villa in the hills, with Count Brode as the Minister in attendance. So the arch enemy, thought Mr. Herbertson, was not in London. And fast upon that thought came the memory of the mad suggestion which had come to him last night. He turned it down instantly, for it was obviously mad. Then he finished the paragraph, which gave some foreshadowing of the Measure by which the Chancellor proposed to heal the open sore of Lusian discontent. Baron Ronnefeldt, the gossip stated, was in residence at the capital, completing his Measure for the Assembly in October.

Mr. Herbertson smiled grimly. The Riddle was still a riddle.

The breakfast hour over, he went to his study and spent two useful hours in completing an essay and one more hour in a lighter task. Margaret Joan was having a birthday shortly, and he was preparing a gift in the form of a water-colour drawing. He gave a few touches to the drawing, which was almost completed, and wrote the letter which was to accompany it. And in this busy morning he almost succeeded in forgetting that outside world which had impinged so rudely upon his own.

He had planned for the afternoon in the garden, and in due course began a vigorous attack upon the disorder which had reared a hundred arrogant heads during his period of unrest. For a time all was well, but presently he became conscious once more of Hadfield's house. He felt that it was again staring at him mutely through the neatly curtained windows of the rooms occupied by the refugees from Lusia. He fumed at the foolishness of it, but the discomfort persisted. Again and again he thrust it aside, again and again it returned. He resolved that he would not look up, but the impulse became irresistible. He looked, and his morbid fancy actually traced an expression upon the senseless back wall of that house, with its innocent windows! It was watching him with a kind of ironic amusement as he tried to underpin his tottering world. It seemed to say Fool! Fool! It seemed to be thinking composedly of The Mills of God.

Then he remembered Fear. It was there that Fear dwelt, to issue forth and stand at his elbow. Yes, Fear!

James Herbertson knew what Fear meant. He

knew the sudden Fear which clutches at the heart
and leaves all the faculties numb, helpless, rudder-
less—a thing so terrible that unless it is removed
it kills. The truth may be calamitous, but Fear
is of the unknown, and no known evil has the
same awful power. How it came back to him now
—that morning in the Prince's house at Graaden,
when a secret messenger had brought the news
that the Saronio plot was discovered, a bolt that
had shattered a thousand illusions and left one confident young fool a pricked bladder! How well
he remembered that cry—"I cannot face him!—
Herbertson, I cannot face him!" and the fever of
helpless rage and regret and doubt and despair.
Then, because even poltroonery must have funds,
he had been forced to go to the Bank with the
Prince to obtain money; and he remembered how
they had waited in the Director's room while that
heavy demand was being considered. That was
Fear. If word had already reached the Bank, the
Director would return, not with the money but
with the police or military. The moments of waiting were an agony. But the Prince's name was
as potent as ever, and the Director had returned
all smiles and assurances. Then the Fear—that
Fear at least—had been dispelled.

One other day of Fear he remembered well,
because it had been the last terror for some years.
It was when he had sat in a Registrar's office, giving the particulars necessary to secure a certifi-
cate for burial. He remembered how he had
watched the man's hand and face as he had filled
in the dates and other particulars slowly, so slowly,
from the slip given by the doctor. Through that

pain of suspense he had yet noticed the tread of a horse's hooves in the street, the voice of a woman singing in the house that adjoined the office. Then the pen had paused in its journey. Discovery?

"Hm," said the Registrar: "Zenandra? Foreign subject? Greek?"

"No," said the man who feared. "Styrian."

The pen had hung suspended for long, long moments. Was the official trying to remember where he had seen that name before? If he tried, a glance at Mr. Herbertson seemed to assure him, for the pen had returned to the paper. No, there would scarcely be any enquiries afterwards. The dead man had no heirs to raise the whisper of foul play and demand investigation. In all respects that really mattered, Adrian Zenandra had died years before that burial. So he had been buried without another question, and the spectre of Fear had apparently been buried with him. Ah, yes, but only to rise again on the Second of May twelve years later, and to take up its lodging in Hadfield's house!

James Herbertson knew, too, the other kind of Fear, for while the Prince had lived there had always been the dread of vengeance by the men whom he had abandoned. They were scattered all over the world, and vengeance has eyes as keen and quick as those of love. Horrible years those, with the shame behind and with a cloud that seldom lifted for a day. He grew hot at the thought of them, with a heat greater than that of the sun beating upon his back.

Mr. Herbertson turned his back upon the house and resolved that he would not look at it again.

He would take care to look the other way, where those new villas had recently been built. They had been an eyesore to him once, but they were a refuge now. They had nothing to do with Fear. He also tried to forget the trouble in a vengeful attack upon the weeds.

But events would not stand still. This time they moved in a woman's call:

"Mr. Herbertson! Mr. Herbertson!"

It was a voice that rang with the gentlest of music. Mr. Herbertson straightened himself, and looked round. It was necessary to wipe the perspiration from his eyes, and when he had done so his vision was still blurred. That, and the music of the voice, and the sudden reaction from the thought of Fear—all these contributed to the foolish impression he received. For she stood looking over Hadfield's wall, and the sun, playing upon her dark hair loosely coiled, had discovered gold in it, and had made an aureole of the gold. She wore white, too, quite an ordinary garment, no doubt; but the effect was so sudden that he might well be excused his ridiculous impression that he saw a goddess in the garden!

"Mr. Herbertson!"

He came to himself—an extraordinary self to come to. He wore heavy shoes caked with earth, his oldest trousers, frayed and soiled, an ancient tennis-shirt, once cream but now a streaky, dirty yellow, and a shapeless hat which had lost even its band. His sleeves were turned up above the elbows, and his hands and arms up to those elbows spoke eloquently of a man who had been "getting down to it." At any ordinary time you would have guessed a gentleman in James Herbertson, but now!——

But he came to himself. She had chased away the spectres, and it was the beautiful afternoon of the twenty-second of May. Hastily he raised that old hat, realising acutely that it was ridiculous, and, replacing it, became aware that the goddess had a faint smile upon her lips and in her eyes.

"Oh, good afternoon," he said hurriedly. "I am so glad that you have come out. I hope it means that your mother is better?"

"Mother is asleep, Mr. Herbertson. She has slept much more since I gave her your letter. So when she slept I wished to thank you for it. And Mrs. Jenner sent me here."

Mr. Herbertson wiped his face: he also drew down his shirt-sleeves and buttoned them. The effect was not noticeably better, but something was pleasing him greatly, and he did not mind. It was not the rather deliberate speech with the Lusian accent, it was not the directness and sincerity of her manner, it was not her smile, or her hair, or her undeniable grave beauty. It was everything.

But it was necessary to reply, and he did it with a start. "I am glad to have your good news," he said, "and I am glad to see you out here. Of course, you could not come before."

"No," said Rhona simply. "But now I had to come and thank you as soon as possible. She wished it."

Mr. Herbertson smiled. "Not the slightest need for that," he said. "Perhaps I should have asked earlier, but of course I did not know."

There was a pause, then, while they stood with

the wall between. Curiously enough there was no awkwardness in the pause for him, nor did she seem to be aware of any constraint. She stood and looked at him frankly, gravely, from eyes that seemed to him to be the homes of many marvellous colours and a whole constellation of stars. In that very brief pause, however, he had time to consider, revise and generally approve his first impressions of the girl. Certainly she was beautiful, though the beauty was of a somewhat grave type. Perhaps recent events were partly responsible for this, but he knew of another reason. She was a child of a large land, where immense pasture plains were bounded by equally immense forests, and the forests rose from height to height into the hoary fastnesses of the Carpathians: and she was of the old Lusian type, imaginative and poetical. The man experienced a definite pleasure in the picture she made, and the artist in the man was equally well pleased.

But it was time to break the pause, and he broke it without any unseemly awkwardness. "Well," he said, "now that you have come, you must see my garden. That door is only secured by a bolt, and the bolt will open easily."

She obeyed with a smile that charmed him. And as soon as she was through:

"Before we speak of smaller things," he said, "let me mention the subject of my conversation with Dr. Henslow. The Countess, he tells me, has been suffering from a constant nervous apprehension."

"It is so, Mr. Herbertson. It is a deadly fear. And it was growing greater every day—till your letter came."

Fear! But it was curious to see how the shadow had passed from the mind of this man, so lately haunted. His manner had a suggestion of iron in it.

"We must do our best to dissipate it, and at once," he said. "When she is well enough I will see her; but in the meantime I wish you to assure her, definitely and finally, that she has nothing to fear. You are both safe here—safer than if you were in your own home at Cronia. Your enemy is harmless."

There was something in the tone that stirred her more than the assurance. She looked into his face with a curious intentness, and her skin grew darker as some thought brought a flush to her cheeks and temples. "Oh," she cried at last. "It is good to hear this. We are, then, quite safe? He cannot enter this house?"

"He cannot," said Mr. Herbertson firmly. "Be assured of that. And now let me show you my garden. . . ."

The goddess followed him as he parted the encroaching branches before her: and there was apparently no spectre of Fear to lurk behind them, or by evil whispers to awaken dark memories in the man's heart.

Mr. Herbertson's garden was a very considerable item to the residents in Arran Terrace. It was naturally large in their landscape, but it was also a standing jest and a perpetual problem. Their neighbour loved gardening so well that he desired a large garden. That was not unreasonable, but why did he not employ a gardener occasionally, and so secure better results? The task was too heavy for any man singlehanded, even if he had abundant time. Few of them understood that it was the employment and the pleasure that mattered, not the results; and there were fewer still who could appreciate that view of the situation.

To-day's visitor, moreover, was a guest from another world, and Mr. Herbertson knew what a garden would imply for her. He watched her with keen interest, therefore, and at once admired the care she used to avoid any remark, any gesture, that might seem to convey disparagement. She recognised her favourite flowers with delight, and it was with delight that she made the acquaintance of some blossoms more at home in England than in Lusia. The tangled incompleteness she found charming also, and seemed to assume that Mr. Herbertson had it so because he liked it so; and she wondered at the variety of rose-trees in his rose-garden without noticing the weeds that rioted between. This tactfulness was fortunate, for she was herself responsible for some of those weeds. So as they explored the wilderness of beauty and non-fulfilment, its owner became more and more conscious of gratification. Seldom had his garden given him such an hour as this.

They explored all, and at last found themselves at the heart of all, to pause before something that was obviously incomplete, a pile in which glass, timber and brick were mingled in confusion. Rhona had seen something of it before, from her window, but at close quarters the mystery was still more of a mystery. She looked to her guide, but he had forgotten his duties for the moment and was surveying the mystery with distinct disfavour. The girl naturally took her cue from his expression.

"Why, it is a ruin," she said. "Did it happen in a storm? Was it struck by lightning?"

Herbertson started, and awoke. "A ruin?" he echoed. "Why, this is a building. It is my new greenhouse."

There was a pregnant pause. Rhona would have framed a swift apology; but then Mr. Herbertson saw humour in the situation, and laughed more heartily than he had done for many days. The mistake was excusable, as he admitted somewhat ruefully. There had been a small greenhouse in the centre of the plot at the time of his purchase, but he had scorned it as something far too small. He had, therefore, commenced a new one on the same spot, leaving the original erection still standing, and laying the walls of the other all around it. It was now three years since he had begun, and he had progressed so far that the walls were up, and even the main beams of the roof. But those main beams, having been exposed to the weather for a considerable time, had lost all appearance of freshness.

"Indeed," said Mr. Herbertson critically, "a stranger can hardly be expected to know that it is a still unfinished work. And sometimes I am afraid that it will really be a ruin before I have finished it. Come and see—but take care of that hole."

What he referred to was apparently a deep pit dug near the proposed doorway of his new building, and partly covered by a plank. It was the pit which had trapped the emissary from Doveton's. "My plan is," he explained, "to have a subterranean room for my new greenhouse—a place of protection for delicate plants during the winter. I have begun it as you see, but—"

He had apparently begun everything at about the same time, and the result was chaos to any one but himself. His present visitor, however, heard his explanations with an interest and appreciation that charmed him.

"I have worked alone," he said, with even a trace of enthusiasm. "And it is a large task for one man. I hope, however, to have the sides put in this summer. They are rebuilding the Primitive Methodist Chapel near by, and I have bought these two old windows. When once they are put in place I shall have made real progress."

The girl was puzzled at times. How could it be otherwise? The whole situation was so new to her. But it was not the situation only; it was the Man. She listened with keen interest to a saying such as that, weighed it, and wondered, her wonder expressed in her glance, frank, confident, yet doubtful, as if she were bewildered by some inexplicable inconsistency. But her bewilderment did not issue in reserve or hesitation. It was rather a stimulus to interest.

As for the Man, the hour was for him one of sheer delight. It was an experience for which he had been ill prepared by his neighbourly appreciation of Marjorie Hadfield, his love of childhood's charm, or his artistic pleasure in perfection of form and colour. Here was trust, too, and reliance, very gracious items to one who had no trust in himself; and here was life, vivid, glowing, resplendent, in the most attractive form that life can offer a man.

His soul felt the warmth and radiance of it, slumbering and stifled elements in his nature woke, stirred, and stretched out eager hands. When she was not looking he found himself watching her face in profile, the round of the chin, the full, sensitive lips, the heavily lashed eyes, the brows as straight and noble as those of a goddess. He studied the colours all unconsciously—the red of the lips, the dusk of the cheeks, the golden sheen of the hair; and then, suddenly, he was in a tremor of confusion, for she had turned to look at him. He could not remember what he had said last, he had not heard what she had asked.

Poor Mr. Recluse! He was paying the ordinary, inevitable penalty of his too quiet and retired life among his books and in his garden. But it was no ordinary person who made him pay it.

Then all too soon came Mrs. Jenner, to say that his tea was ready. A whole hour had gone! When he realised it he was astonished, and it was almost in silence that he escorted the girl back to Hadfield's door. It never occurred to him that she might have been asked to share his solitary tea. At the door she turned with a smile and held out her hand.

"You are very kind, Mr. Herbertson," she said.

"Oh? Am I?" stammered Mr. Herbertson, foolishly. And she smiled again, with something more definite than a smile dancing among the stars in her eyes.

"You are very kind. And I want to tell you, Mr. Herbertson, that we shall have no fear now that you have told us. We shall feel absolutely safe."

"And you are safe," said Herbertson, positively. "Never have a shadow of a doubt of that. You are perfectly secure."

("Liar!" whispered some mocking spirit in his consciousness. "Curse you, it's no lie!" retorted another Mr. Herbertson, in fierce defiance. "It is true! It shall be true!")

They faced each other for a moment. Their hands touched. Then with another smile she passed through the door and was gone. . . . After a while he closed the door and turned towards his own house. He went slowly, but not in the depression of recent hours. His step was light, and he actually hummed some stray air of music as he passed through his study.

Before he washed his hands he found his *Telegraph* and re-read the Styrian Letter. It confirmed his recollection of the first reading. Then he consulted a time-table with great care, and changed his dress, putting on those grey tweeds in which he had gone up to London on the Second of May. Then he went down to tea.

In a few minutes the watchful Mrs. Jenner came in with the teapot and a dish of hot cakes. She noticed his attire at once, but had scarcely done so before he announced his purpose.

"I am going up to town after tea, Mrs. Jenner."

Mrs. Jenner laid down the plate which she had brought in. She laid it down suddenly.

"Going up to town, sir?" she said.

"Yes."

"But that will be the second time in less than a month, sir."

Mr. Herbertson looked up, a little surprised. "Why, so it will," he said. "What of that?"

"Oh, nothing, sir. It is a pleasant break for you, and I'm sure you need such."

She went out, leaving him to his tea. She tried to enjoy her own, but the attempt was not a success. Mr. Herbertson was going up to town a second time within a month! His last visit had resulted in the arrival of two foreign ladies, who were very well in themselves but a portent which could not be disregarded. More than that, Mr. Herbertson had never been quite himself since that time, and in various details the old order of steady work had been broken. The garden showed signs of it, and Mrs. Jenner guessed that her employer's desk would show signs of it too. And now he was going up to town again!

Mrs. Jenner had an intuition that something was happening to a very pleasant world. She had a stake in that world, and was afraid. Twelve years ago she had lost her husband, just after his elevation to the rank of Inspector in the local police, and had been left with an allowance insufficient for her maintenance though useful as a contribution thereto. For two years she had lived with a married son, but sorely against the grain of her independent spirit; and then Mr. Herbertson had come, and had solved her problem. With wisdom very quaint and uncharacteristic, he had gone to the police station of the district, and had asked the Inspector in charge to recommend an honest and efficient housekeeper. This Inspector, successor to Inspector Jenner, had at once named the widow of his former chief, and Mrs. Jenner, allowed to have certain of her cherished household possessions for her own use, had become an inhabitant of Mr.

Herbertson's refuge with joy and relief, for behind her lay two years of trying semi-dependence, and all about her a world in which there was much want and much uncharity. So the fair, stout little woman with the silver hair and the simple heart gave thanks continually for her good fortune, and gave thanks all through the day by unremitting regard for her master's interests. . . . But always at the back of her mind lay the fear that something might happen some day. As her relatives had often said, this was too good to last!

Now, on reviewing the events of recent days, she knew that there was cause for disquiet. As she pondered her heart grew heavier, for she realised her helplessness. Between her and her master there was every confidence and kindness, but there was also some barrier which she could never cross; and these mysteries were in his world, not in hers. She could not even ask a question. What could she do?

She did what she could. She heard Mr. Herbertson prepare to go, and met him in the hall.

"You will be tired when you come home, sir," she said. "Shall I get you something nice for supper?"

Mr. Herbertson smiled. "All my suppers are flawless. But what is in your mind, Mrs. Jenner?"

"A tender chop," said Mrs. Jenner, "and an apple-dumpling, boiled."

"It is a very kind thought," said Mr. Herbertson. "Would the apple-dumpling be good for a late supper?"

"With my making it couldn't do harm, sir. And you don't usually go to bed directly after supper."

"No," said Mr. Herbertson, "I do not. And I am obliged by your very kind thought. I shall look forward all the evening to my supper."

He found it easy to be gracious, one of the facts that made the happiness of Mrs. Jenner. Somewhat comforted, she cleared away the tea and in due course set about her preparations for the special supper, her last task being that confection of Devon which she regarded as the pearl of all her cookery lore. She made Mr. Herbertson his apple-dumpling, and having made it, set it aside carefully for boiling. And as she set the white ball on the dish, she regarded it admiringly. Its satisfying roundness pleased her, and she made a reflection which she always made on similar occasions. "Round, like the world," she thought. "Round, like the world! Fancy a pudding being like the world!"

Mr. Herbertson was touched and amused by the incident. His errand was enough to occupy his thoughts, but vagrant musings on the subject took him to Mrs. Jenner's halting-place and further. "There must be symbolism somewhere in this," he reflected. "I wonder what it means to her. After all there is a good deal in an apple-dumpling. It is a sphere—a world: and, like the world, it is rich in its contents . . . the apple, in itself a symbol of life and love; and at its heart the seeds of other spheres, too numerous to count. . . . Why, it is not only a symbol of the world—it may be regarded as a symbol of eternity—the life that continually reproduces itself. But I believe that Mrs. Jenner removes the core of the apple—no doubt all good cooks do. So there the likeness ends. Here, then, is one world that will not repeat itself. . . ."

Then Mr. Herbertson placed a rein upon his fancy. "You are out upon a perilous errand," he sighed, "and yet you waste your time in evolving a philosophy of an apple-dumpling. Will nothing bring you to your sober senses? I wonder if Philip will!"

Chapter IX

Count Brode Gives Ten Days

ARRIVING at King's Cross, Mr. Herbertson took a taxicab to the Petersburg and so reached that Mecca of the world some time before dinner. In the great hall of that magnificent caravanserai which looks down so placidly upon the Haymarket one might have imagined him more than a little awed by the retinue of splendid beings who lingered in groups at various points of vantage; but the Petersburg is known for its courtesy to inconspicuous strangers, for in a house where you may meet a reigning sovereign on the stairs any unknown may prove to be a personage. So when Mr. Herbertson made his enquiry he received immediate attention, and presently one of the splendid bodyguard took his modest slip of pasteboard upstairs. . . . It bore, in addition to his name, *"On urgent business."*

Mr. Herbertson waited amid the splendour as unobtrusively as possible, wishing that he were anywhere but at the Petersburg. He had hoped that Philip Brode might not be there, and now he hoped that he would refuse to see a stranger; at the same time he hoped that he would get the interview, and handle things so well that his wards in Arran Terrace might rest in peace. He did not believe, however, that he could handle the interview efficiently, and he dreaded the clash of hostile minds, violence of speech, a blunder in tactics, some ridiculous failure that would mean disaster. All these apprehensions were simple and definite, largely the outcome of his own disposition, but there was another more formidable than all. Circumstances were forcing him to walk in dangerous places, and he heard a persistent whisper—Fool! Fool! Fool!

His present doubts were soon determined. The splendid attendant reappeared with the message that the gentleman was in and would see him; then he led Mr. Herbertson to a lift, which discharged them presently on one of the upper floors. Here on another splendid but less peopled corridor he tapped at a door, opened it, murmured "Mr. Herbertson, sir," and left him within the threshold, closing the door behind him.

Philip Brode had been reading an evening journal, and was standing in the window. He turned as the door was opened, curious to discover who this stranger with urgent business might be. Mr. Herbertson had known, of course, that he would meet the man he had seen in the cemetery. He saw the same face, the only difference being that the features were not now illumined by that species of evil triumph which had been so noticeable on the first occasion. Without this illumination, however, they seemed heavier and older, coarser, more animal, with the Tartar strain much more clearly marked. The man was little over thirty, but his was a life in which every passion had moved unchecked. He was dressed for the evening, probably for a theatre. "A powerful young man" would have been a first-sight verdict, but an examination of the features would have suggested a change. He was a very powerful young savage. Mr. Herbertson had seen this before, but now he saw it at close quarters. He thought of the girl whose profile he had so lately seen in a garden, and experienced some sudden emotion which appeared to have the effect of strengthening his purpose. He advanced into the room quite boldly.

Philip happened to be in an easy humour, and curious. What he saw was what all saw who looked at Mr. Herbertson: a plainly dressed, middle-aged and unpretentious man, though undoubtedly a man of refinement and a gentleman. After the first glance, however, he knew that they had met somewhere before. Moving forward to a table, he laid his paper down and looked at his visitor questioningly and with a dawning suspicion.

"Good evening, sir," said Mr. Herbertson plainly.

"Good evening," said the other, with a slight inclination of the head. "You wished to see me?"

It was a sufficient opening, and Mr. Herbertson took it. "Yes, sir," he said; "I have come as a friend of the Countess Hamar."

The younger man waited with a look which became intent. This Englishman spoke with a directness which he could appreciate. Mr. Herbertson returned the look and proceeded to explain:

"Circumstances," he said, "brought me into contact with the Countess some days back, and I learned the whole story—the incredible story—of her misfortunes."

In that opening Philip recognised an attack, and was put upon his guard. His face darkened.

"I had known Count Hamar," said Mr. Herbertson, in the same tone, "and I felt it a privilege to serve his family. At my suggestion the ladies left London and went into the country."

"Ah! So it was you!" said Philip, abruptly.

Much to his own surprise, Mr. Herbertson felt no fear at this unmasking of the batteries. In his next words his voice rose to an aggressive and threatening note.

"Yes," he said. "It was I. I am glad that I have had that honour. But I find, sir, that these ladies are still being pursued by those whose treachery has brought them to ruin. And I have come here, sir, to demand an assurance that this persecution shall cease. Otherwise—"

There was a pause, full of wrath. Philip's temples were crimson, and it was only with difficulty that he forced a question. Considering the circumstances, it was politely phrased:

"And—and who the devil are you?"

Mr. Herbertson did not blench. "That is my business," he retorted. "Your business is with my message, not with me. I have asked for a certain assurance. Unless I get it, and at once, I shall take other steps to obtain it."

So far, good. Mr. Herbertson was encouraged by his enemy's speechlessness, and rushed at his next sentences.

"The Hamars shall be protected. The incredible story of their unmerited sufferings, of the treachery which has betrayed them, and of the vile persecution which has followed them even in their exile, shall be given to the public. And I warn you, sir, that when these things are known there will be no roof in London to cover the men responsible for them."

Philip was staggered. Earnestness had clothed his accuser with a certain indefinable dignity, and this had found an ally in the stilted phrasing of his long-conned protest. Philip was enraged as well, and his face was a study in wrath: but Mr. Herbertson went bravely on to round off his rehearsed address.

"As for the effect of that story in Styria, sir, you may know better than I; but I am very sure that it would be read with great interest there."

Again a tense pause, while the eyes met and fought. Philip was bewildered, alarmed, furious, and he was not accustomed to hide his emotions. That dastardly betrayal had been accomplished in the dark, but here was a man who had discovered the secret and would expose it to the world. Perhaps he could not prove it, but truth does not need much proof. . . . Besides, there were so many envious souls who would be only too ready to believe! Herbertson felt his detestation of the man gain force with every moment, and suddenly it reached a climax. The quiet man angered usually rushes to extremes, and he was an imaginative man as well. Looking straight into his enemy's eyes, reading the passions that played there, he recalled the face of the girl in his garden, and saw some sudden flashing picture that fired him to madness. So he lost all control and broke through every barrier of convention with an epithet which had not been rehearsed.

"You filthy brute!" he said.

It was so low-toned as to seem a confidential communication, so fierce and tense as to seem a blow. To Brode it was much more than a blow. He could have answered a blow, but this was beyond instant reply. He stood rigid, amazed, speechless, as though in one devastating moment his soul had been stripped naked to the public gaze. Nor did his first conscious thoughts help him. What did this man know that he could speak in this way? Guilt and fear wrestled with his rage. And Mr. Herbertson, seeing his guilt and fear, ceased to wonder how he had come to utter that unpardonable epithet. He stood undaunted, unshamed by his astonishing outburst, and free at last from the shackles of formal and stilted language.

"You refuse?" he asked resolutely.

With an oath, Philip made a step forward. His very natural inclination was to take his visitor by the throat, shake him like a rat, and then hurl him through the window. Utterly at a loss, he could not vent his anger in words. As far as he knew it would be necessary to find English words, and his command of that language was not sufficiently complete to suit moments of emergency. Mr. Herbertson did not stir.

"If I go," he said, strongly, "I go straight to a newspaper office. Do you really understand that?"

He waited a moment for an answer. Then he calmly picked up his hat from the table as though about to leave. He turned towards the door, and paused. That last thrust had been a vital one, and the angry young man's countenance was a picture of bewilderment and discomfiture. He seemed to be searching for a reply that would not come. Suddenly he turned and walked to the window.

Several moments passed. Philip was plainly at a

loss, and Mr. Herbertson saw victory within his reach. He cast about for a remark which should force matters to a triumphant conclusion. Perhaps he had done enough already. Perhaps he had achieved his purpose. But it would be well to get some word of assurance as a trophy. He would give the man—well, he would give him another thirty seconds.

Probably there are few things that may not be decided in a mere half-minute.—life and death, happiness and misery, failure and success. The man who plays lightly with it has failed to realise the infinite possibilities that lie in little things. Now it was something from outside that changed the situation. As they waited in tense silence, they heard some one pass up the thickly carpeted corridor and open a door on the other side. Mr. Herbertson took no notice, for footsteps had passed to and fro at intervals since he had entered the room. But the younger man listened, and then he turned with a gesture of menace.

"Wait for me here," he said. And without pausing for a reply he strode to the door, threw it open, and left the room, closing it behind him. Apparently he crossed the corridor to the room which some one else had so recently entered. Then silence fell.

This movement had taken the visitor somewhat by surprise. Naturally his thoughts flew to seek an explanation. Some one had entered a neighbouring room, and Brode had gone to consult that person. Who could it be? With the question came the answer, for only one answer seemed possible.

The minutes that followed were apparently anxious ones to this would-be protector of women. He passed them in a state of indecision, now rising to move to the door, now taking his seat again to wait. To go was to throw away everything for which he had come; to stay, said hope, was at least to have a chance. He was not quite certain. Yes, he must wait. So he waited. It might have been three minutes, it might have been ten; but the man who waited was scarcely the man who had so forcefully delivered his ultimatum just before. Indeed, he decided at last that he would not wait, but go; but when he had reached this resolve it was already too late. He was not the man for rapid decisions.

Footsteps again in the corridor, again the opening door. Philip Brode came in, bringing with him the person he had gone to consult. Mr. Herbertson was not facing the door as they entered, and he did not attempt to move. He remained standing at the table until they both paused before him; but it was in vain that he strove to appear composed and self-possessed.

"This is the man," said Philip in Lusian; and the newcomer looked at Mr. Herbertson attentively. He was a man of something over sixty, but not an old man in any sense but that of age and experience. A mass of silver hair was brushed back from clean, transparent brows, and the white, beardless face showed the lines graven by strong feelings and deep thoughts; but the physical and mental vigour of the man was unimpaired, for every movement was quick and alert. The cast of the features was hawk-like, and the glance of the keen eyes under heavy black eyebrows had that quickness which marks a wakeful and watchful mind. Moreover, if there was one thing to be read in the man's manner more clearly than others, it was that he had the power of perfect self-control. He might be a man who never hastened, never spoke without thought, never acted without a plan, a master of self and of circumstance.

He looked at Mr. Herbertson searchingly. No one could have guessed from that look that they had ever met before, for in addition to his natural gifts Count Brode had received the useful training of a diplomat. In a moment he moved to the table, and took up a card which lay there. It was the visitor's card.

"So," he said gently. "Mr. Herbertson. On urgent business." And then he resumed his scrutiny.

It was a tableau which might have appeared to mean very little had it not been for the extraordinary attitude of Mr. Herbertson himself. That gentleman had never recovered his calmness, but now stood pale and mute, a picture of discomfiture. And the Count was one of those who do not need words when they can read the signs. In the other man's face he saw the key to a somewhat unlooked-for situation and grasped it without hesitation. He saw that he was master, and having seen this, had little need to enquire how or why. He would discover everything very soon.

"This is an unexpected pleasure," he said, suavely and with great deliberation. "I could not have hoped to meet you in this way, Mr. Herbertson. I did not know that you were in England."

Mr. Herbertson made no reply. Philip stared at the two in surprise that gradually developed into satisfaction. His fear had gone. To him the Count turned next.

"You tell me, Philip," he said, "that Mr. Herbertson, having fallen in with the Hamars—apparently by accident—has taken them under his protection. Is not this the case?"

Philip nodded acquiescence. The Count went on slowly.

"I am bound to admit, Philip, that Mr. Herbertson has some right to intervene. It is true that he knew the unfortunate Hamar, and may even claim to be regarded as a friend of the family. On the other hand, I cannot admit that he has addressed himself to the matter in a regular and gentlemanly way. He has been harsh and even violent. He has threatened you. He has spoken to you of the newspapers, and of public opinion in England?"

The young man nodded again. He was not swift in conclusions, and the dramatic change in the situation had bewildered him; but when his father had taken matters in hand he could be patient. And the Count proceeded with the same deliberation. He had already seen appeal in his victim's eyes—the dumb appeal of the culprit who fears to be dragged into the light; and he began to see a means of prolonging the man's torture and making his own triumph more complete. Quickly the germ of a cruel plan took form in his mind and was approved. As he spoke so deliberately he perfected it.

"Mr. Herbertson, you have been indiscreet. A man with a past such as yours is surely indiscreet when he threatens an appeal to the public. Nevertheless, I admit your right to intervene, and the form can be amended. Philip, in spite of his ill-chosen method of approach, this gentleman is a man of honour, and he knows Styria and its customs.

He will no longer speak to you of the public. He will take another way."

"And that way?" asked Philip, puzzled.

"The way we have in Styria when two men find themselves in dispute over—well, over a woman!"

As he reached that point his features seemed to grow more distinctly hawk-like in their cast, despite the fact that there was a slight smile upon his lips. It was the face of one who loves cruelty for its own sake as well as for the purpose it may serve. As he spoke his fingers played idly with the intruder's visiting card.

Mr. Herbertson made some effort to recover his dignity; but though he opened his lips, no words issued. Then he made a movement as if to turn, but a careless gesture from the Count seemed sufficient to check him. The indignant and heroic Englishman of the previous scene had left a very inadequate substitute.

"What! The duel?" cried Philip, with sudden intelligence; and his father nodded. His scheme was growing with every moment that passed, and it became more and more attractive as it grew. He also became more and more sure of his mastery. Some amazing chance had delivered an enemy into his hands for destruction: but there must be torture before destruction.

"You understand, Mr. Herbertson," he went on carefully. "This is a much more interesting way out of our difficulty. It is, further, the only way we can accept after the manner of your intervention. You may be sure, however, that we shall abide loyally by the result. Let me, then, state the conditions. You will meet Philip under the usual rules of the duel.

Should fortune favour you, my son withdraws. Indeed, we promise this—that he will withdraw even if the meeting has no definite result, feeling that you have, by meeting him, established your claim to make a rule in this matter. But if fortune should favour him, I take it that you will no longer stand in the way."

There was no emphasis upon the last words, and only the man addressed could see their diabolical meaning. Mr. Herbertson saw it, and was stirred to an effort to recover self-control. He spoke with dry lips. His voice was little more than a whisper.

"And if I do not care to—to fight?"

"That," said the Count, seriously, "is certainly a possibility to be considered. But if you refuse, you will surely see that it is impossible for you to meddle further. This is your opening. If you take it, whatever the result no one shall know of your story. If you refuse, there is the public! And one might speak to the public of you, Mr. Herbertson, with some effect! One might ask the public to enquire"—he leaned forward and ended his sentence in a lower tone—"to enquire *how your master died.*"

Mr. Herbertson was clearly incapable of an answer. A minute fled in silence—a terrible minute; then the Count, as if a little weary, a little disgusted, ended the interview.

"That is all, Mr. Herbertson. We shall wait a few days for your decision—let it be ten days, for you shall have time to think. If you do not accept in ten days, we shall know that you will not stand in the way. If you accept, we can make all further arrangements then. That is all."

That was all. The master-player had said it,

and it was final. Mr. Herbertson turned, and moved towards the door.

"Your hat, Mr. Herbertson," said the Count politely, "is upon the table. And your gloves."

The victim paused, fumbled for the articles mentioned, and picked them up. Then he went hurriedly to the door, passed into the dusky corridor like a man half-blind or half-intoxicated, and so towards the stairs. The older man opened the door and held it for him, bowing with grave courtesy as he passed through. Then, after closing the door he joined his son at the window, smiling at his own thoughts, perhaps at the recollection of Mr. Herbertson's appearance in departing. His son searched his face in bewilderment.

"And what does it all mean?" he asked. "What has that man done?"

"It is quite simple, surely," said the Count. "He is a criminal. Could you not see the guilt in his face? My dear fellow—"

"Yes, yes," cried Philip, impatiently. "But what crime? Is it a serious one?"

"No doubt people exaggerate the seriousness of murder, Philip, especially in England. But still—"

"Murder? That man? It cannot be!"

The Count smiled. He enjoyed a contest with this slow mind just as he enjoyed other pursuits with a spice of cruelty in them. But he always remembered, soon, that the slow mind was his son's, and withdrew.

"Suppose it were poison?" he suggested. "Many quite gentle souls have turned to that species of murder."

"Poison? Ah, I see!"

"You shall see more in time. But that is not the point just now. The matter has a very personal aspect, as you will have guessed. Many years ago two young men affronted me very gravely. It was before your time, Philip, so it is not necessary to repeat the whole story. The offence was so grave that only one punishment could be adequate. But there was no opportunity. I lost sight of those men, and after a time one of them died. The other has been here this evening. It is clear, I think, that he did not expect to meet me. He thought to meet only you, who would not know his past and whom he could threaten. He would not have come to face me. No."

Philip slowly worked his way to a question.

"But you have allowed him to fight," he said. "You have given him a chance."

"There is no chance," said the Count.

"There are always chances in a duel," persisted Philip, wise in his own province.

"Not for him. He will not face it."

Philip was silenced, but still bewildered. After a pause, however, his father gave him a little further light.

"I have often wondered, Philip, how the fish feels when it is on the hook. An interesting question! Probably the creature feels little, because it has few sensations. But a man—with a man it is different."

Philip did not see the application at once, but it came, and his heavy face lightened. But his father passed on.

"You have not asked my news," he said. "Indeed, you have had no opportunity. This interruption—so unexpected, yet not unwelcome—no, no, not unwelcome. But I have spent three days with the Emperor, and I have used them well. I made various representations in view of Hamar's death and the fact that his daughter cannot be held responsible for her father's disloyalty; and I have the promise that if she becomes your wife the confiscated estates shall return to her—or rather to you."

"Then you succeeded?"

"Do I ever fail, Philip? Your surprise is a little ungracious. Yet I forgive it, because it is also a compliment. Yes, I succeeded, and now you hold a strong hand. You cannot hope to win at once, of course—the wounds are too fresh. And we must admit that our measures have been drastic measures, let us say exceptionally drastic! But given time— time, time . . . and the inevitable pressure of circumstances—and patience and tact, Philip. . . . Well, I will supply the tact—while you wait in the background. No, no, you must not hasten the wooing. You are too abrupt, forceful. You must leave everything to me."

The son considered. In the next sentence he revealed himself.

"Up to a certain point, yes. But after that I will see to things myself."

Their eyes met, leering evil in the one face, appreciation and contempt mingled in the other.

"Each to his taste," said the Count. "We need not go into details. To you the girl is desirable, to me Cronia is worth while. Our aim is to secure both: but even if we do not get the girl we have established a reversionary interest in Cronia.—And now comes the pleasant interlude of our Mr. Herbertson. How did he discover the women?"

"Just as we did, I suppose. The name on the cross. I saw him wandering in the cemetery."

"This is very interesting. It is also amazing. So he is 'protecting' the Hamars! Disguised as a gentleman! What a situation!"

He gazed out across the Haymarket, but without seeing anything of London. He saw, instead, a most diverting mental picture. His son tried to see it too, and thought he succeeded.

"Of course they don't know," he said. "It will be a shock to them when they learn the truth. Curse them!"

"We have cursed them," said the Count, turning back from the window. "And it seems that there is more yet. The cup is not full. Fortune is very kind. She is providing surprises for my later years. Some very pleasant ones. Well, this interlude of Mr. Herbertson will occupy us very agreeably for a month or so."

"And I am to kill him after—if he comes?"

"Of course."

"And if he does not come?"

"I shall deal with him in some other way. It will not be an easier way for him. I shall not lose him again!"

"That is satisfactory," said the son, shortly; and in his consciousness a certain epithet burned a little less fiercely. But he did not tell his father of that epithet. There are limits, and he kept this shame to himself.

Meanwhile the Champion of Dames returned to Waldington. All through his journey to King's Cross, and afterwards in the train, the voice which had cried "Fool" was engaged in the pleasant refrain, "I told you so—I told you so," and he had no reasonable retort to offer, nor any defence. Disaster, however, had provided one definite result, and when this emerged from the welter of shame and dismay the man was able to recover some degree of self-control. When he reached Arran Terrace at last it would have needed a keen eye indeed to discern any traces of a devastating experience.

Mrs. Jenner's eye was anxious, but it was not sufficiently keen for that. Mr. Herbertson had returned, and that was the main thing; he was quite normally cheerful, and that was well; he asked about his supper at once, which seemed to suggest that all else was well; and he sat down to it presently with clear signs of appreciation. The shadow which had hung over the house all the evening was dissipated, and Mrs. Jenner sat down to her own supper with genuine relief. The peril seemed none the more imminent for this mysterious journey.

She did not know. In the dining-room the Champion of Dames looked with a rueful expression at his housekeeper's comely *pièce de résistance.* Even in this depth of disaster Mr. Herbertson could not resist an outcrop of his quaint humour. "Yes," he said, with a sigh which had some amusement mingled with its pain. "Mrs. Jenner always removes the cores. So it was a true symbol. This is a world which will not repeat itself. This is the end!"

Chapter X

Mr. Herbertson Leaves His Garden for the Third Time

"SO this is the end!" said Mr. Herbertson, unaware that it was really only the opening scene of the Third Act.

It was the morning after his visit to the Petersburg. He was sitting at his writing-table in the study, considering a course of action. In the course of many years' leisure he had acquired some trifling habits which betrayed a man of abundant time and of a methodical turn of mind. It seemed to him that his thoughts were never so clear as when he was alone in his own room, facing his garden, with a pen in his hand and with a sheet of paper before him. It might not be necessary to write, but it was always well to be ready to jot down any point which might seem worthy of special attention. Under these familiar conditions the mind seemed to work more easily.

Mr. Herbertson seldom covered that garden outlook, even in the evenings when the room was lighted. He liked to have his outdoor realm not only visible but accessible, and all his writing was done with his face to the window. This habit provided some amusing incidents in his daily life, for even a slight pause in the process of composition would end in a curious diversion. He would take a walk in the garden in order to find the phrase he wanted among the surroundings he loved best; but when this happened it was quite likely that his desk would be deserted for the rest of the morning, some other task having caught the wandering attention. On the other hand, the phrase would sometimes come when Mr. Herbertson was busy with spade or fork: then he might be seen hurrying up to the house to fix the fleeting treasure with pen and paper before it should elude him. Then at lunch time Mrs. Jenner would find her master busy at his desk in his garden clothes, with the forgotten spade standing reproachfully at the door.

In this case, however, the preparations were unnecessary. The night had intervened, and he had had time to consider his position in all its aspects. Even then it had been simply a matter of confirming the conviction which had come to him as soon as Count Brode had met him face to face. In his heart he had said then, "It is all over," and now he found nothing left but to write it down. No, it was not even worth while to write it.

He laid down his pen, therefore. The question "When to go" was easy to answer—he had Ten Days—but it was rather difficult to decide upon a place. Of course he need not leave the country. It had many towns like this town, and in the course of time he might obtain a garden even more satisfactory. If he did not care to stay in England, he had the whole world to choose from, with the definite exception of Styria—the East and the Far East, the great continents of the West, the new lands under the Southern Cross. And it was not likely that such an encounter as this would occur more than once. The Brodes would never cross his path again. Indeed, they had not crossed his path now. He had crossed theirs, in spite of his clear intuitions of danger. Fool! Fool! Fool!

He was in the depth of his bitter reverie when Mrs. Jenner tapped at the door. "Here's the young lady to see you, sir, if you please," she said; and as she turned away Rhona came into the room.

Mr. Herbertson rose at once, a different man. "This is a pleasure," he said, with his customary urbanity. "I did not hear you come into the house. Will you take this chair?"

He was quite surprised by his own change of temper. One quick glance around his bachelor den seemed to set her at her ease, but she did not take the chair. She had only come to bring a message.

"Thank you, Mr. Herbertson," she said. "I must not stay just now. I have only come to tell you that my mother is much better this morning. And Dr. Henslow tells us that it will not be hurtful for her to see you."

Mr. Herbertson was a little taken aback. He was being plunged again into the heart of that adventure to which he had just written *Finis*. Yet in a moment he recovered himself and accepted the situation. What else could he do? Refuse?

"I am glad to hear this of the Countess," he said cordially. "It will, of course, give me pleasure to come. Shall it be this morning?"

"Could you come in half-an-hour?" she asked, almost eagerly: for to her there was joy in this appointment. It was so clear a sign of progress.

"Certainly. Let it be in half-an-hour."

That, apparently, was all her business, and she turned to go. Yet even as she turned she spoke:

"Mr. Herbertson, is it yet too soon to expect any good news?"

Mr. Herbertson rose to the occasion, for the occasion was an appeal. "My dear young lady," he said, "I was only wondering whether I should tell you now or wait until I came in. Last night I went up to London, and saw the man to whom you owe so much anxiety and misfortune. I had the pleasure of pointing out to him the danger of pursuing you further."

There was utter surprise in the pause that followed. It was an emotion dangerously flattering to Mr. Herbertson. When Rhona realised what he had said her eyes glowed.

"You saw him?" she said wonderingly. "Oh, Mr. Herbertson! You went to see him—for us? And what did he say?"

"He had little to say," answered Mr. Herbertson, promptly. "In fact he was greatly astonished to find that you had a friend in England. Moreover, he saw clearly that there was trouble in store for him unless he ceased his persecutions. I believe he realised, at last, that England is not Lusia."

The girl listened with flushed cheeks and parted lips, and her eyes—how amazingly expressive! "Oh," she said quickly, "that was good. And will he trouble us no more?"

Apparently Mr. Herbertson, so easily led out of the paths of truth and prudence, found the descent fatally easy. He spoke as a man with authority, one who had gained by achievements the right to speak. Poor fellow!

"I want you to believe," he said, "what I have already told you—that you are quite safe here. I want you to leave your security in my charge. Can you do so?"

He smiled as he put the question. Rhona, however, did not smile as she gave her answer. She looked him steadily in the face. It was a searching look, yet confiding too. And how stimulating!

"Yes, Mr. Herbertson," she said simply. "I believe that we can." And then she moved to the door, and he opened it for her. These interviews ended with noticeable abruptness.

When she had gone he returned to give calm consideration to what had passed. And as he recalled it he was not a little astonished.

"Good Heavens!" he murmured, "what have I said! And what on earth made me say it?"

There was no answer to that question save the usual answer—"You are a futile person, James!" But this was so adequate that he hadn't the heart to seek another.

He passed the interval in a somewhat abashed and confused state of mind, and went into Mrs. Hadfield's with no clear idea of what was to happen. That little lady met him on the doorstep with a beaming face.

"They are expecting you," she said. "She is sitting up, and seems ever so much better. Isn't that good news?"

"Indeed it is," answered Mr. Herbertson. "I am very glad that I brought her to such a capable nurse."

Mrs. Hadfield laughed, well pleased. She led him to the stairs, and there Rhona met them.

"I heard your voice," she said.   And then in a whisper:

"It must not be more than ten minutes."

Mr. Herbertson nodded.   He followed her up to the room, and in a few moments was face to face with the invalid.

Yes, the Countess was better.   She was sitting up, propped by her pillows and wrapped in some fleecy covering which Mrs. Hadfield had been able to supply.   Nevertheless, there was nothing of the great lady in this broken-down and wasted woman whose life had met so sudden and so awful a disaster, and whose anxious and sunken eyes looked out now from a worn and pallid face.   Herbertson saw that she had lost much since that day in Franklyn Crescent, and his face was sufficiently sober.   Henslow had spoken only just in time.   He was no alarmist.

She greeted him with a smile—a smile of gratitude!   For a moment he was a little embarrassed, but he took the hand she extended.

"It gives me much pleasure, Countess, to see you growing stronger," he said, as he took the chair that awaited him.   "I trust that your recovery will now be rapid."

As he uttered that banal remark he found himself regarding the situation with considerable surprise.   Rhona had gone to the other side of the bed and had seated herself there, holding her mother's hand; and the two women were looking at him together, eager for every word that should fall from his lips.   They rested their hopes in him absolutely—in him!   Oh, wonder of circumstance, what but an eccentric Providence could have devised such a situation as this! Was he the man who had awaked one morning to remember that it was the Second of May, and that a parcel was due from Stoughton's?

"Mr. Herbertson," said the Countess, weakly, "I am glad that I can see you, and thank you for all your kindness. It is what I have wished to do."

Mr. Herbertson thrust the wonder into the background. Otherwise conversation would have been impossible. He protested, earnestly, that there was no need for thanks, but he ceased as she held up her hand. She must not be agitated by protests.

"Do not deny me," she said. "Now I hear that you have done still more. You have seen him."

"It is true," said Mr. Herbertson. "I have seen him." And a return of confidence enabled him to add. "It seemed necessary, Countess, that some one should meet him on your behalf. And I took that liberty."

"Liberty!" said the Countess. "But what did he say? Tell us again."

Mr. Herbertson was obliged to be equal to the occasion. Well, he had created it himself from one point of view, and from another point of view he must play up to his eccentric Providence! He answered bravely:

"He had little to say. His conduct, indeed, was not to be defended. All that I demanded was an assurance that he would trouble you no more."

The Countess flushed and her eyes brightened. "That was good," she said. "And then?"

"He was silenced," answered Mr. Herbertson,

"as I have said. Finally, it was arranged that a definite answer should be given within ten days or so. I have no doubt as to what that answer will be."

"Ten days?" cried the Countess. "I know what that means. It means that he will take time to consult his father. Plainly, the Count is not in London."

Herbertson was silent. He had no love for lies.

"I feel sure it is that," she went on wearily. "The young man can do little of himself, evil though he is. It is the Count that is the brain and soul of this wrong."

Then a sudden anger rose in spite of her weakness. A flush crept into her lined and pallid face, a light came into her eyes.

"If you have ever seen Count Brode, my friend— and perhaps you saw him when you were in Styria— you have seen a man who has only one motive in life—self-gratification. He is not one of the beasts of the field, however; he is much greater than that, and his desires are of another kind. Power is one of them, and wealth another because it means power. He has others, among them cruelty and revenge; but he has those gifts which enable him to conceal the motives of his life—even for years—when it is profitable to conceal them. Mathias never knew him until the end came. I knew, but he would not credit it."

Herbertson seemed to see in that last sentence a whole history—the quiet woman in the background watching with growing uneasiness the man who came in and out as a neighbour, and beneath his suave exterior reading unerringly the things that governed him; and while her warnings had passed unheeded, the shadow had grown darker, the cloud had covered the sky, and she had found all she loved swept away by the storm.

"He has made enemies," said the Countess, "but only those that he could afford to make. Never was an evil man more prudent. Once he fell under the Emperor's serious displeasure, through a quarrel with Prince Adrian; but that was the only time he took a false step. It was so perilous a lesson that he would not be likely to forget it. When the Prince fell he crept back into the sunshine, and there he has remained since. His political services have been considerable. And he is so old and wise now that I cannot think he will ever make a mistake again."

At that point a slight constraint fell. The Prince's name had fallen without thought, and the Countess observed at once that she had touched delicate ground. She went on quickly:

"You met Count Brode. Did you know him at all well?"

"Yes," answered Mr. Herbertson. And after a moment he added, "I, too, fell under his displeasure. As you know, I served the Prince."

The Countess seemed to be trying to remember, but the effort was too much and she gave it up with a sigh. Presently it would come.

"Ah!" she said, "is it so? Then I fear—I fear that he will hate you after this. He never forgives, never forgets. He is a man who never abandons his hatred!"

She seemed troubled by the thought, or by the memories it brought, and Herbertson watched her anxiously. But in a moment her face cleared.

"Yet what can he do to you?" she asked.

"Against you he is powerless. You are an Englishman."

"And that is a great deal to say," agreed Mr. Herbertson, rising to take his leave. "I am not alarmed! But for the present, Countess, your mind will be at rest. Do all you can to recover your strength. Much may happen in ten days."

Hope returned to her worn face. "Yes," she said. "And we shall hear something soon from our friends in Styria."

Herbertson left her without saying what he knew: that even their most faithful friends in Styria would not dare to lift a finger to assist those whose names were marked with the leprosy of treason. Indeed, there was nothing in his attitude at parting to suggest a doubt of a swift and happy solution.

For the hour that remained before luncheon he walked in the garden. He found it necessary, poor man, to reconsider carefully the whole situation. It had been settled already, and "The End" had been written; but it had been written too soon. He was not free to write it. Now he must turn back those last pages and read them once more. Where did he stand? What was to be done? What could he do? "You have forgotten something," whispered that eccentric Providence. "Indeed, you have forgotten many things! And they are important. Suppose we go over them again?"

He saw that three courses were open to him as a result of the interview yesterday. They were these: first, he might refuse the duel, maintain silence, and let the Count do his worst; second, he might retire from this affair altogether; third, he might accept the challenge.

This being clear, he looked for the results of each course, beginning with the first. What would happen if, refusing the challenge, he allowed Count Brode to take his own way? What way would he take? "One might ask the public to enquire *how your master died!*" The answer was clear enough, and Mr. Herbertson did not take longer to consider the conclusion than he had taken to arrive at it. That course was absolutely impossible.

In the second place, there was the plan he had already decided upon. He might retire altogether from this unfortunate affair. He could go away, taking what he could take, leaving what he must leave. He could begin again elsewhere, for with his disappearance the Brodes would serve no purpose by betraying him. This, as he saw at once, was a simple and easy course. It even seemed a natural one to take, and an hour ago he had definitely accepted it. But now Mr. Herbertson looked at it and turned away. Those poor women!

Drawing his hand across his brow, he turned to the last course. He might accept the challenge. Yes, there was that amazing alternative, so amazing that he had not given it a moment's consideration until now. But there it was, and he actually proceeded to examine it. *He might accept the challenge!*

He recalled the whole of the circumstances under which it had been given. He recalled the expression of his enemy's face, his very tones, in the endeavour to grasp his motives. In this way he arrived at certain conclusions.

It was plain, in the first place, that the challenge was an unnecessary step on the Count's part, for

Mr. Herbertson had been sufficiently in his power in any case. That is to say, he need not have placed his victory in this affair on the hazard of a duel. Knowing the man's nature, Mr. Herbertson felt sure he had been led to this step by two arguments. One was his conviction that the challenge would never be accepted; the other was a greater reason, probably the governing reason. Hate—the Hate of the Brodes, almost a proverb in Lusia for years past. And here was a pretty psychological problem which our philosopher examined with wonder.

"Yes, it is true," he decided at last. "What the wise men have said about Hate seems to be justified, though it is hard to believe it. Why, it is like love— it is stronger than death. It is so strong in this old man that he would probably take risks to gratify it. Even he, usually so cautious, so calculating, so wise! He would take risks!"

This was a remarkable conclusion, but he was inclined to accept it. "Yes," he decided, after further thought. "He took the risk of giving me a chance, knowing that it would be torment to me. That's it, exactly. Tantalus! He dangles a rosy hope before me, and knows how I must suffer in reaching after it. Having me in a tight place, his sentence is 'Ten days' torment'—And then disappearance—or perhaps worse! With a parting kick he clears me out of the way—and takes all. Oh, Count Brode, it was very neat of you—very!"

His artistic soul admired the neatness of it, but could find no comfort in it. Indeed, he found cause for rage in it.

"But of course he takes no real risk," he reflected a little more soberly. "He seems to take a risk, but there is no real risk. He knows me! But if I were another kind of man, Count, you should pay for this! Unfortunately I am my accursed self, and you are in no danger!"

That conclusion led to another, equally unsatisfactory, and he was amazed to see how the dexterity of the old man revealed itself afresh at every turn. "But even if I were another kind of man, and went to face him, I should still lose," he thought. "I should quite certainly be killed, and they would have the field to themselves. And even if by any miracle I were not killed, I should be quite as helpless as I am now. They would not keep faith—not for a moment. . . . I should still have to vanish. And then—"

Feeling himself hopelessly outmanœuvred by this master-player, he spent some time in trying the situation from another angle. It would be very satisfactory to be another person and to accept the challenge . . . but to be shot would make it an expensive satisfaction. His life would be thrown away for nothing. For nothing.

There seemed to be no doubt about that, but somehow his mind disliked the "Nothing"; and because it disliked it, he found himself attacking that conclusion with a feeble resentment. For nothing? Why not put in "Something" instead? Suppose he decided to throw away his life. Was it possible to purchase Something by the sacrifice?

(He, James Herbertson, to think of sacrifice in connection with himself! Yet here was a problem, and it is a function of the human mind to attack problems—for its own sake, if nobody's else's.)

Restitution—that was the word that emerged at

last as the solution to be sought. Restitution for these women. Suppose he were willing to sacrifice his life to restore these women to their home. How could it be done? And since it is seldom that one word comes without bringing another in its train, he presently found himself with two words. Restitution—Remission—Remission—Restitution. "They are synonyms in this case," he reflected. "I have resurrected that wretched curate and his text. 'Without the shedding of blood there is no Remission.' 'Without the shedding of blood there is no—Restitution . . .' Oh, damn the curate! And why can't I turn to something else?"

But he could not turn to something else, and even the question worked to increase his discomfort. "Turn" suggested a turning of that troublesome text, and a moment later it had taken a form still more irritating. *"With* the shedding of blood there *is* Restitution . . ." And when he reached that point he went to his garden as a refuge, and worked violently for a useless hour. For that changed text stood at his elbow, as the shadow of Fear had stood on another day, and gave him no peace; and Hadfield's windows looked out upon him with a bland silence through which one word seemed to ring like a clarion: "Restitution! Restitution! Restitution!"

He gave it up at last, and accepted the problem once more. Well, let it be so. At least he might work it out and see what form the solution might take—if there were a solution. *"With* the shedding of blood there may be Restitution." But—how? . . . And he had not faced that naked question for three minutes before the only possible solution was plainly set before him.

It came suddenly and vividly, with all the surprise of a new thing; but it was really a natural outcome, the next step on the road he had been pursuing. As it came it left him breathless, so great was the shock; and from that instant he ceased to play with his problem, for it was a matter of life and death.

"Ah!" he said at last, under his breath. "If that might be done!"

His first impression was that the thing was impossible. It seemed to him the wildest and most absurd of a series of absurdities, only to be dismissed instantly with ridicule. But because the suggestion was a natural outcome it refused to be dismissed, and grew more and more a thing to be considered. And the man found himself considering it, with hands clenched and a face graven deep with lines of pain.

The course that had suggested itself was the only one that offered hope; but it surprised him that he had ever conceived the idea. Another man might have done so, but he knew his own weakness, and he could not conceive that weakness should bear such fruits.

Now, having realised that this course was the only one that offered a hope, he came face to face with the question, "Can I?" And here again he suffered a surprise, for when he began to look into his resources it did not seem that the venture lay so entirely beyond him as he had imagined at first. He did not try seriously to discover the influences which had worked the difference. He ascribed everything vaguely to the fact that he had passed the age when life is valuable for what it may give in the years to come. There was nothing to live for—then why not a useful death?

Nevertheless, that hour before luncheon and another hour that came after were a time of conflict. At times he had sense of terror, for there must be terror in the realisation that the impossible thing is the only thing possible, the hopeless course the only hope. But finally he chose this course and communicated his decision to Rhona in a brief letter. For the only hope of doing this thing was to commit himself to it at once.

"A plan has occurred to me as a consequence of our talk this morning. I have a friend or two in Styria who might use their influence if appealed to in person. I propose to go over immediately and see them."

He sent this note in by Mrs. Jenner, and then consulted his time-table. As he did so he reflected upon the tragic manner in which his adventure was developing. The first unconscious step had been taken on the Second of May, and now he was contemplating a journey from which there would be no return.

When he had chosen his time he began to make the other preparations which an orderly mind finds necessary under such circumstances. These were interrupted by a visit from Rhona, a more girlish Rhona, flushed, excited.

"You are going to Styria?" she cried breathlessly. "And for us? Is it true?"

No one could have imagined that he had done so much problem-solving within the last hour or two, so easy and assured was his manner.

"I have quite decided upon it," he said. "Indeed, it is rather surprising that I did not think of it before. I am not entirely without friends there, and I can at least try them. And of course an interview is much more satisfactory than a letter."

"And when do you go?"

"I must leave this evening."

The girl looked at him intently. He feared that she might penetrate beneath his mask and discover how momentous his project was. As it happened she only read him imperfectly.

"You will be in no danger in Styria?"

"Oh, no," he replied at once. "There will be no personal danger for me. You may rest assured of that."

It seemed to satisfy her. He noticed that she placed implicit faith in what he told her, and remembered that she had done so from the first. He was pleased. To a self-distrustful person the faith of another must needs be grateful, even when it is embarrassing. He began to feel that the task he had undertaken was less difficult than it had appeared to be. But that was an illusion, he decided at once.

"I am glad of that," she said. "I—my mother— would be distressed, Mr. Herbertson, if through us you should suffer any—any loss. Now I will go and tell her, and if she has anything to say I will come in again."

When she had gone Mr. Herbertson took the opportunity of completing his preparations. It was necessary to give his housekeeper some explanation. He did not realise how much his words meant to her.

"Mrs. Jenner," he said, "I am going up to town,

and it is quite likely that I shall be away for two or three days, or even longer. But not more than a week, I hope."

Mrs. Jenner heard in silence entirely unusual with her. She did not even look into his face.

"When I am gone," proceeded her master, "it is quite possible that enquiries may be made for me, and it is very important that you should not give any information whatever. My destination, in particular, must be kept a profound secret."

Mrs. Jenner was silent still. Profound secrets—in Arran Terrace!

"I know," continued Mr. Herbertson, "that the house will be safe in your hands—and of course there are our friends within call. The important thing is that no one outside shall know where I am gone. You will not forget this?"

"No, sir," answered Mrs. Jenner at last, but without her usual eagerness. "I won't whisper it to a soul. But the ladies next door—I suppose they know?"

"Oh, yes, they know. I was referring to outsiders. Thank you, Mrs. Jenner. I shall feel quite easy in my mind now."

Mrs. Jenner departed, without even asking her master where he really was going. She did not discover this until he had gone, but it did not seem to matter. She had no doubt, now, that her Dreamthorp days were numbered.

Shortly afterwards Rhona returned. "I have told my mother," she said. "She begs that you will not place yourself in any danger. Any other cost which may fall upon you she will be able to repay later, but she could not repay that. And she is grateful—oh, so grateful—for your so great kindness. That you know, even if I did not say it."

The girl was agitated. Mr. Herbertson noticed this with a vague pleasure.

"Do not entertain the slightest fear for me," he said confidently. "And I shall be sufficiently repaid if I find the Countess better when I return. And now, what is that slip of paper? Is it for me?"

He took it from her hand. "It has the names," she said, "of some few of our best friends. If your own should fail, these might help."

He examined the brief list rapidly. "It was a good thought," he remarked, as he folded the paper. "You must trust me to make the best use of my journey. And now I think I must say good-bye. In ten minutes I shall be gone."

He took her hand. He was one of those staid and sober men who never forget their age, and who even exaggerate their soberness a little when they are in contact with those younger than themselves. In the present instance he was not only an elderly friend, but also the adviser and protector. Fancies about goddesses had no place just now. Afterwards he took her to the door, and then in a matter-of-fact way made his own private comments.

"She is a splendid girl. What a life she would lead with Philip! I wonder if he would give up for a week—if he had her—his other women. I think we must do our best to save him from such a problem! And now for those names again."

He opened the paper once more, and read the hurriedly written lines. Then he tore the slip into fragments and threw them into the waste basket under his desk.

"If the only hope should fail," he said, "and I am laid by the heels, that list might play the devil with several people. Our friends place us in danger so thoughtlessly!"

A few minutes later, after carefully surveying the street from his window, he left the house and made his way to the railway station.

Chapter XI

Mr. Herbertson Interviews a Statesman

THAT third journey of Mr. Herbertson from the shelter of his garden was remarkable in its manner and surprising in its end. In certain details it must needs be like the journeys of other men, for he was obliged to use the ordinary means of transit and to submit to their unavoidable inconveniences and indignities. In these matters he acted with a normal intelligence, securing his passports and selecting a fast boat-train to Dover without mishap, but never had a traveller crossed the Channel and Europe with so little regard for incidents of the crossing. He acted as a man might have acted in a trance, spoke to no one save under the strictest necessity, partook of food without observing it, exhibited no signs of disappointment or irritation under hindrance or delay. The pier, the steamer, the voyage and the landing on the other side were but phases of a panorama which was hastening to some unspeakable climax. Paris was but one dim and fleeting stage of a journey which had nothing to do with Paris, other cities came and passed with their inevitable roar and babble and illumination, but throughout he seemed to be sitting in a corner of a compartment with a paper before his unheeding eyes and all his faculties bent blindly upon a purpose which would not bear scrutiny or description.

It was afternoon when he arrived at Graaden. He did not know the day, but he remembered distinctly that he had hoped to arrive on the Wednesday afternoon. Therefore this was probably Wednesday. He left the station in a hotel carriage with a party of American tourists, and presently found himself alone in a small room which overlooked at a great height the beautiful Square of Saint Catherine, with the old cathedral set like a cool, brown shadow of the past in the glare and glamour of the new day. There he took a little rest, and did not attempt to stir abroad until dusk. He even had refreshments brought up to his room instead of seeking them at the public tables.

When he thought it sufficiently late he went out and made his way to the southern quarter of the city, avoiding the more public thoroughfares, but, nevertheless, meeting with no difficulties as to direction. He crossed the magnificent Place of the Eagles, with the great mass of the House of Assembly on the north side, and turned into the long avenue of white houses which opens into it on the east. And at one of these he stopped, undisturbed by the scrutiny of a police officer who had casually moved in his direction.

Mr. Herbertson of Waldington was actually paying a call at the official residence of one of the first statesmen of Europe. Without hesitation he went up the broad white steps and rang the bell before the massive door which seemed so immovably closed. The police officer passed slowly and silently, but Mr. Herbertson gave him no attention. He waited with every appearance of calmness until the door was opened by a uniformed man-servant. To him he told his purpose in the Styrian tongue and with businesslike brevity.

"His Excellency," said the servant, with equal brevity, "is not receiving callers to-night."

Mr. Herbertson paid no attention to the final nature of the statement. He had not expected miracles and had come prepared for such a reception. He now produced a sealed note.

"His Excellency will consent to see me," he replied firmly. "Be good enough to give him this."

The man was surprised, not so much by the reply as by the manner in which it was spoken. There were certain varieties of manner among petitioners and place-hunters, but this was not one of them. In his surprise he hesitated.

"My business is urgent," proceeded Mr. Herbertson, in the same tone. "Let there be no delay."

By that time he was standing in the hall, with the door half-closed behind him. His assurance, perhaps that uncharacteristic dignity of bearing which he had somehow conjured up for this crisis, had the effect he desired, and the man called a fellow-servant into consultation. Presently this person took the visitor's missive in a gingerly and indifferent fashion and disappeared. It was some three minutes before he returned, but then the question was settled.

"Will you come this way?" he asked respectfully. "His Excellency will see you in a few minutes."

Those few minutes were spent by Mr. Herbertson in a small anteroom, where he sat quite alone. Whatever his business might be, it was evident that the Chancellor did not wish to give his servants any impression of its importance. After that time the door opened again, and he was told that he would be received. Following to another door, he was at once ushered silently into his Excellency's presence.

Baron Ronnefeldt, the Chancellor of the Empire, was a man of fifty, a strong man who had fully proved his strength. He had distinguished himself by the way in which he had brought order out of the chaos of Styrian home politics, especially with regard to the open sore of Lusian discontent; but in this he had been greatly assisted by his courage in dealing with foreign affairs. At the very outset of his reign as Chancellor he had faced a crucial test with such boldness that he had won the esteem of the whole nation and the respect of all Europe. In him Styria had found a Man, and even the Lusian irreconcilables could respect a Man. They were now awaiting his Measure with grim resolve but with definite apprehension.

At the time of Mr. Herbertson's entrance he was dictating to a secretary, and he did not pause when the visitor crossed his threshold. He stood at the table looking down upon the paper, a somewhat large-framed man with broad shoulders and iron-grey hair, and with a profile whose ruggedness was eloquent of power. The last sentence was written and the third person silently left the room; and it was not till then that the Chancellor turned to Mr. Herbertson.

When they came face to face the contrast between the man of large affairs and the obscure gardener-essayist was decidedly pronounced. After one silent look the Chancellor picked up from the table a slip of paper. It was the note which the visitor had sent in to him. When he spoke his voice was even, his manner untroubled. He did not offer a seat.

"Mr. Herbertson," he said, "from England?"

The visitor seemed to be reassured by that question, as though he had feared an unfriendly reception. He advanced a little.

"Yes, your Excellency."

The Chancellor glanced at the paper again.

"You have written a name here, sir—the name of a man dead. And you say that you come upon his business."

"Yes, your Excellency. I felt that I must use his name for the purpose of gaining this interview. Yet that was not a stratagem, for it is certainly upon his business that I come."

The Chancellor glanced at the paper yet once more. Then he tore it across several times with great care, his plain, strongly-cut features still inscrutable.

"Yes," he said. "That name would naturally command my attention. Then what is your business, Mr. Herbertson?"

So far all had been introductory. Mr. Herbertson had been bracing himself to his task while the statesman had been considering the ground. Now the visitor lost no time in approaching his point, and used little diplomacy in reaching it.

"It is this, your Excellency," he said. "I have come from England on behalf of two ladies—exiles from Lusia. I speak of the Countess Hamar and her daughter. I have an appeal to make to the

Emperor, and I ask you to procure me an interview with his Majesty."

There was a long pause. The Chancellor gave no indication of surprise or of any other emotion. Mr. Herbertson added an explanation:

"I fell in with the ladies by accident," he said. "They needed help, and I could not refuse it. Your Excellency probably knows that Count Mathias died in England only a few weeks ago."

The Chancellor nodded. It was soon clear that his mind had remained with the chief question.

"An interview with his Majesty," he said slowly. "Mr. Herbertson, I must speak plainly in the beginning, so that argument may be unnecessary. The thing is quite impossible."

Mr. Herbertson, however, was not discouraged. In a surprising way the man was rising to the occasion. "Pardon me, your Excellency," he went on earnestly: "only the greatest necessity makes me ask it. My purpose is to save two innocent and helpless women. It is not a small thing that I ask, but on my part I am willing to pay the price. And it is a considerable price for any man. I am giving my life!"

There was no sign of answer, but there was no time. Mr. Herbertson continued his story.

"My intervention will be fatal to myself. That is of no importance to any one—indeed, it will only close a dark chapter which no one will wish to read again. And as I have said, I am willing, or I should not be here. But I must say a word for these women. It is all I ask—that before I give up my life I may say a word for these women to the man who can help them. And what I ask of you, Chancellor, is to give me the opportunity of saying it."

There was something of hysteria in the haste, urgency and emotion of the appeal. The listener was certainly impressed. His face did not lose its sternness, but the answer which came at last was unexpectedly gentle.

"Can you not leave their case with me, Mr. Herbertson? Why trouble his Majesty?"

But even in the face of that half-promise the visitor persisted:

"I would see the Emperor. It is necessary that I should see him."

There was another pause, but the Chancellor did not ask the reason of this persistence. He knew. It was not for nothing that he had passed through and controlled great crises, reading the minds of men more surely than they knew them themselves.

"Mr. Herbertson," he began, in the same even tones, "I desire to speak to you as your friend, for the sake of the man who was once my friend. I would say to you this: It is well that that man is dead and forgotten. Let him rest in his grave. Do not, I beg, bring up his name now to trouble one who has suffered so much and must be troubled no more."

Mr. Herbertson lost his air of urgent assurance. He seemed to shrink from the penetrating regard of the speaker's eyes. He faltered. And yet there was undoubtedly something in the voice that helped him to recovery and to a new persistence that was less assured but not less earnest.

"I ask for one opportunity," he said hoarsely.

"It is impossible."

"Your Excellency, I ask for one chance—for the sake of that man who first took you to the Emperor, and so brought you to this place. May I not believe—may I not plead—that his memory claims it from you?"

The Chancellor stood like a wall. He spoke with sudden sternness, as if to rebut an implied reproach.

"There is a claim, which I acknowledge. Let me tell you, sir, that I remember that man every day with a prayer for his soul's peace! But there are other things before him."

The answer was intended to be final. As it was spoken the Baron turned towards the table to reach a hand-bell. Up to this moment he had been standing on the hearth, with his back to a shaded lamp. But at that movement Mr. Herbertson made what must have been his last appeal.

"Your Excellency! Six-and-twenty years ago I saw you stand at the altar of Saint Catherine with your bride. She was one of the purest and best of women. For the love you bore her, I ask you for this chance to save a woman equally pure and good!"

Ronnefeldt had his hand over the bell. He had paused, apparently to hear the sentence out, and when it had been uttered he still stood as it were in the act of striking the call. But no sound came. He remained standing over the table for two or three moments, as if something had suddenly occurred to give him pause. Then he stood upright, and looked at Mr. Herbertson once more.

That gentleman met the glance, but he made no further appeal. Apparently he had shot his last bolt. The two men stood for a while eye to eye in a painful silence. Then the Chancellor gave his answer:

"Mr. Herbertson, I am willing to give this matter further consideration. But I must have time. Will you come to me again in the morning?"

The pleader was breathless, incredulous. He could only stammer his reply:

"Certainly, your Excellency."

"Then do so—at eleven o'clock. But I must have your promise that you will then accept my decision without cavil."

The visitor acquiesced in silence. He had no time to examine the condition. His face was beaded with sweat.

"And where are you staying?" asked the Chancellor. "The Hotel St. George? That is very good. It is where many English stay. Then I shall see you in the morning."

The interview was over; but instead of calling the servant, the Baron himself conducted the visitor from the room, and then led the way from the hall down a small corridor to a side door facing a deserted street.

"This is a private way," he said. "To this door you may come to-morrow."

That was all. Mr. Herbertson passed out, and the door closed silently behind him.

When he had gone the Chancellor returned to the room in which the interview had taken place and sat down at a table, his face heavy with thought. In a while the secretary came in, and laid before him several papers which he read and signed. When this was done he rose and passed out of the cabinet by a heavily curtained door at the end of the room.

Within was a smaller chamber, a retiring room for his own use. Plainly but comfortably furnished, it had a certain atmosphere of domesticity. The books here were not official volumes but his own books, and several articles of furniture suggested the rule of a woman. A woman had arranged it, and he had made no alterations since she had left it for the last time five years ago.

Here on many a troubled evening he had found her in the intervals snatched from the tasks of the outer room, and here they had sat together for an hour when the secretaries had gone and the night was still. And here she still reigned for him, for it was her portrait that hung upon the wall that faced the hearth, a life-size painting by the best brush in Europe.

He went up to the hearth now and stood there, gazing earnestly upon the face of the faithful woman whom he still worshipped in spirit. Theirs had been a perfect union, but though this was well known there were none who could guess how much of the success of his public life had been due to the one who had sat with him hour by hour in this room. And if the thing had been asserted while she lived, no one would have been more surprised than she.

"I wonder," he said slowly, "if that is the secret. I think it must be."

Then his thoughts turned to the great crisis of ten years ago. He had come in from the cabinet one night with his mind on the rack of indecision and doubt. The Turkish Ambassador had just left him, his mouth filled with promise and prevarication, and he knew that to-morrow would open with no advance made through the maze of a fruitless negotiation. His course was clear in his own mind, and he was free to take it; but there was a paralysing possibility of failure, and he suffered that dread of a false step that, while it perpetuates ten thousand wrongs, prevents a harvest of wars. Before he could take his course he must have something which it seemed that no one could supply.

Then he had come into the smaller room, to find her sitting there reading. In a listless and weary irritation he had told her the whole story. She had listened with her grave eyes upon his, but that silent look had acted like wine upon his jaded spirit. Even before the story was finished his tone had changed, his decision had been taken. Something in that look had given him just that fibre of boldness which was needed for the occasion. She had wondered and rejoiced to see the shadows pass away, little thinking why they had passed; and as soon as his story was done he had gone back to the cabinet and had written the despatch which for decades all Europe had longed to write.

Next morning the Turk came again, to meet no arguments now but a plain severity which he took to be only another phase of the endless round. He had gone away, smiling and well satisfied; but in the late afternoon he had returned: this time he had no smiles.

"Your Excellency," he said, "I have received a telegram. Styrian warships in the Mediterranean are moving to the East. There appears to be a combined movement."

"It is true, Highness," answered the Chancellor.

"I need not remind your Excellency that such a movement may be misconstrued. Manœuvres in those waters are surely not desirable in the present strained condition of the public mind."

The Turk did not try to hide the menace in his protest, though the suavity of his manner could scarcely have been excelled. The Chancellor answered very briefly:

"Your Highness is under a misapprehension. These are no manœuvres. The fleet will reach Salonica to-morrow at noon."

The silence that fell was tense. Haran Pasha's swarthy features hardened. He did not smile again for many hours. He almost lost his diplomatic manner with his next remark:

"Your Excellency realises that such a step can mean only one thing."

The Chancellor bowed. "Much as I regret it," he replied simply, "I have been obliged to prepare your Highness's passports."

The Turk sat, his gravity the mask for his bitter confusion. He was beaten. What had this man behind him, that he could have taken such a course? Was it an intricate intrigue with the other enemies —one so deep and skilful that he had failed to suspect it? Was he simply a fool, or was he an extremely strong man—strong enough to act madly when he saw occasion for it, and strong enough to face the consequences?

There was the one chance that this was a last move in the great game, but he dared not trust this chance. Salonica—by noon to-morrow! He thought he could hear the roar of the first gun—

the sound that would bring down like a house of cards, in every market in the world, the laborious and precarious edifice of Turkish credit. It might do more—it might break that spell of enchantment under which the Crescent had been allowed to rank among the standards of the West for so many years. No man could say what that first gun might not shake down.

With an unmoved front he rose and went out; but the long contest had been won.

The Baron remembered every emotion of those anxious hours which had made him famous. Best of all he remembered the look which had given him the steel of victory.

"I wonder," he said again. "I wonder!"

Chapter XII

An Agony in a Garden

MR. HERBERTSON returned to his hotel and mounted to his room. He had neither succeeded nor failed, but he had not broken down. He was surprised, elated rather than depressed, though exhausted both physically and in spirit. He had been battling with a power greater than his own.

Later this mood of elation passed, and he began to see things in their true proportions. More than this, he went to another extreme, as he usually did. The Chancellor had not conceded the boon —he had only withheld his answer. It was possible that he had only put the thing aside in order to deal with it a more convenient way. He had secured his visitor's address, and perhaps this indicated mischief—a visit from a posse of police, an arrest, a prison cell. There were many Herbertsons, but there was one James Herbertson whose proximity should be of interest to certain authorities if they were informed of it.

Mr. Herbertson sat for some time at his open window, which was placed so high that it gave him a considerable outlook. He could see the opposite half of the square, brilliantly lighted and throbbing with the life of the great city. Its murmur rose about him, and he could distinguish the flash of white faces on the thronged pavements. But he could see beyond the square, over the buildings which fronted it on the other side, lighted streets that narrowed into ribbons in the distance, cluster after cluster of illuminated buildings spreading far out in a great half-circle rimmed by the darkness of the night. And it was greatness that he saw wherever he looked—below, the wide pavements pulsing with the life of a far-spreading Empire, and, beyond, the capital of that Empire, thrusting her long avenues into the plain and into the night. But the man who surveyed it all was an obscure man who had come from a small strip of garden in a country town in a foreign land. He had dared to intervene in great matters, had interposed his puny person among men who moved as giants.

He closed the window and turned away from it. The prospect was too large for him. In a little while he retired, not to rest, but to run the tiring circle of doubt and hope and regret until the morning dawned. He had known the Chancellor long, and would not have considered him capable of failure or treachery; but perhaps the Ronnefeldt of to-day, the Ronnefeldt of success, was not the man whom Prince Adrian had befriended so many years ago.

Even if he had not deteriorated, however, he would regard himself as the Empire's servant, and Mr. Herbertson's request would stand or fall on that ground alone. And there, it seemed to the suppliant, he had no chance at all. The pause at the last was mysterious, for Mr. Herbertson could scarcely believe that he had been influenced by the reference to his wife. That had been a forlorn hope. Some idea had occurred to him, and he had decided to reconsider the whole subject. It was in that mysterious pause, that unlooked-for hesitation, that Mr. Herbertson saw his only hope.

He had a wretched time before morning came, and when he went to keep his appointment it was with a hopeless heart. It seemed to him that this world was a nightmare crowded with awful emotions, one agony treading upon the heels of another. At that hour the city was in the full flood of its morning's life, but he hated it all. That little garden at Waldington was the world that matched him best, and the new greenhouse in that garden was a task large enough to have contented him. He had been mad to attempt another. Perhaps he would awake presently and find that he had not attempted it!

When he reached the white house, however, he found that he was looked for. As he approached the private door it opened before him, and a mute servant ushered him at once into the waiting-room. Five minutes more and the Chancellor joined him.

The statesman answered his visitor's greeting briefly, coldly, studying his face as he did so. Then he announced his resolve without preamble or delay.

"Mr. Herbertson, I have decided to grant your request. You shall see the Emperor."

So it was done. But before the visitor could speak—for his surprise was great—Baron Ronnefeldt proceeded, a little abruptly:

"I could not arrange this, of course, without consulting his Majesty. I need not tell you that my task was a difficult one, but finally his Majesty consented to receive you—for a few minutes. Perhaps I need not say that you owe this boon to his Majesty's keen sense of justice."

Mr. Herbertson had obtained his desire, and there should have been relief in his look; but if it was there it was obscured by other emotions. The statesman read his looks without a sign of pity—indeed, with some sternness.

"He will see you this morning," he continued. "And at once. Does that meet your wishes?"

Mr. Herbertson was evidently startled. It was quite clear that the immediate nature of his appointment did not appear to him an advantage. But he recovered himself almost instantly.

"Your Excellency is very good. And I am extremely grateful," he said haltingly.

"Come, then," said the Baron.

Mr. Herbertson followed him in silence. They passed into the gardens of the Chancellor's house, which lay behind the building itself and which were very extensive; for this quarter of the city was of comparatively recent development, and had been generously planned to accommodate the most important State buildings and official residences. The palace which the Emperor occupied during his residence at the Capital was also in this quarter, and was accessible from the Chancellor's grounds. Indeed, Mr. Herbertson's ordeal was very near at hand.

Presently they reached, at the end of the garden, a door, which the Chancellor opened with a private key. A short covered way brought them to another door, where an armed sentry stood on guard. He saluted the Chancellor, who opened this door

in the same way. Mr. Herbertson followed, and
found himself standing in the Imperial Gardens.

They lay deserted in the morning sunshine, silent
save for the murmur of fountains and the mingling
notes of many birds. As they entered Mr. Herbertson had a glimpse of the palace in the distance,
rising white-fronted upon a series of terraces
brilliant with flowers and gleaming with statuary.
It was only a glimpse, however, for his guide turned
into a walk which was sheltered by tall shrubs.
In a few minutes they reached a small summer-
house, standing where three paths converged.

"His Majesty," said the Chancellor, "will see
you here. You will wait until he comes."

He led the way into the building, which was
simply furnished. They glanced round in silence,
and there was a moment of constraint. Then the
Baron faced his visitor:

"Mr. Herbertson," he said, earnestly, "I am
giving much into your charge this morning. Remembering what his Majesty has suffered—and his
advanced age—you will be discreet!"

It was an appeal which seemed to move Mr.
Herbertson strongly. He returned that earnest look
with one of equal earnestness. It was the look
of one who understood.

"I will be discreet," he said.

The Chancellor nodded, turned, and walked
away, taking a path that led towards the palace.

Mr. Herbertson was left alone, face to face with
the greatest ordeal of many years. At the end
there had been no time for thought. Events had
moved with amazing rapidity, but here was an interval in which reflection must have its place.

Reflection was not helpful to him. Indeed, it brought him into a state which promised ill for the fulfilment of his pledge to be discreet. He paced the chamber unevenly, or rather he moved about it stumblingly, now pausing to move a chair, now bending over the table to examine with unobservant eyes the books which were scattered upon it. All the while he strained his ears to listen, and turned again and again to glance furtively at the turn of the path which the Chancellor had taken. And if any of his acquaintances had seen him then they would have found it difficult to recognise him, so greatly was his face aged by mental pain and conflict. There was no sign here of the easy-going philosopher whose chief interests in life were essays and roses.

The minutes passed slowly—all the more slowly, it seemed, because of their stillness; but at length his straining ears caught the sound of footsteps. As soon as he heard them they seemed to strike loud upon the silence. Breathlessly he watched the turn in the path. Then an old gentleman in grey, tall and military in figure but with the unmistakable stoop of age, came round the corner and approached the summer-house.

On that morning the Emperor of Styria might well have been taken for some British country squire making a tour of inspection in his grounds before luncheon. The relaxed attitude, the leisurely walk, the severely simple and unostentatious mode of dress, all suggested a man whose interests lay in the land and the garden, with regimental memories in the background and a seat on the local Bench as one of the permanent features of life.

This impression was only to be dispelled by a meeting face to face, when a single glance would reveal the ruler who for some forty years had worn with stedfast courage and unwavering purpose one of the thorniest crowns in the world. Those high features had all the calm dignity and strength of the Roman patrician, the keen eyes had the lofty and piercing gaze of the eagle. Those who met him could never forget afterwards that the emblem of his Imperial house was an eagle perched upon a rock, daring the sun. Ferdinand of Styria had been given a great part to play in this drama of ours, and every passing year proved that he had the spirit to play it greatly.

He came up the path slowly, looking idly to right and left, and he was within a yard or two of the threshold when he first looked before him. Mr. Herbertson had controlled his nervousness by a great effort. Standing beside the small table, he saluted the Emperor and submitted to a swift scrutiny. After that one look His Majesty sank into a chair. Mr. Herbertson, of course, remained standing, the table between them.

"You are the Mr. Herbertson?" said the Emperor coldly. "And you wished me to receive you?"

Thus he laid down the basis of their relations during the interview. An outsider might have supposed that the old man had never met this petitioner before, or that the wrong in which he had shared was a thing half forgotten; but those who have sinned or suffered know too well that for a great wrong a thousand years is but as yesterday. Yet in a sense the mask was one of mercy, for without it the interview would not have been possible. It provided an atmosphere, though that atmosphere was one of dread.

"Yes, your Majesty," answered Mr. Herbertson.

"I understand that you have some communication to make in the matter of the Hamars. I am ready to hear you."

Leaning back in his chair, he laid his walking-cane across his knees, and waited. But while he waited he watched Mr. Herbertson with eyes which saw everything. That gaze, cold, searching and scornful, was an ordeal from which even a brave man might have shrunk.

Mr. Herbertson could not claim to be a brave man, and he seemed to be severely tried. His story had been to some extent prepared, but he found it difficult to open the first chapter. When he had begun, however, his voice gathered some firmness, though his sentences were sufficiently halting and broken throughout the interview.

"Your Majesty's kindness is very great," he said. "It is true that I come here on behalf of the Hamars. The cause is urgent, or I would not have dared to visit Styria."

He paused, but the Emperor gave no sign. Therefore the halting story was continued:

"Some weeks ago I discovered that the Hamars were exiles. The mother and daughter were friendless and helpless in London, the Count having died there. I found also that they were pursued by the enemy—a relentless and powerful enemy—who had accomplished their ruin already. And it seemed that there was no aid for them."

Again Mr. Herbertson paused. He thought that the Emperor's face had darkened. His own pallor increased, but he showed an unexpected courage.

"Hear me out, your Majesty! There are no slanders in my mouth. All that I have for you is the truth. I—I have nothing to gain." And after a moment he went on:

"The knowledge came to me in a strange way —so strange a way that I was almost forced to intervene. I found that a sin of other days was bearing fruit, a sin committed by a man who must be nameless before your Majesty, a man whom death has removed and whom no one would wish to remember. But his sin lives on, in the ruin of these helpless and innocent women. And I believe that it is not too much to say—of that man—that if he had lived to this day he would have seen it his duty to do for these unfortunates anything that he might be able to do in atonement. But he could do nothing, and the duty seemed to fall upon me, his companion and fellow-conspirator. It was— it seemed to me that it was—a legacy. . . . I offered the Countess a shelter, and gave her my—my protection."

Mr. Herbertson faltered at that word. He believed that a suggestion of a smile passed over the grey mask of his listener's face.

"Her enemy, however," said Mr. Herbertson, "still pursued her, and found her. He also found me, and when he found me I was in his power because he knew a secret of mine. Also he hated me for an old cause, and it was not his nature to forget. So as he could do with me as he would, he resolved to kill me unless I left these victims at his mercy. That was my choice—to go away and save myself, or to stand by them and suffer death."

The tones of the speaker now struggled against an increasing huskiness.

"Your Majesty will believe me when I say that my course seemed clear! What could a mean-spirited man do but escape? But, sire, a single hope came to me in the darkness. I said, 'What would that dead man do? What could he do in my place? Had he but a spark of manhood left, he would surely wish to make some atonement to these women. Nay, he would feel that his life was a small thing to give if he could undo some small part of the old wrong.'"

The Emperor sat, a man of stone except for those merciless eyes. Mr. Herbertson fought with his huskiness and found clearer speech.

"He could not have the opportunity. It was offered to me, and to me alone. Might I not take his place? A life is still a life. It is the utmost that I have to give—it would have been his utmost too. And I said that I would give my life—not gladly, because I am not a brave man—but I would give my life if it would serve these women. As far as I could, I would take his place.

"But how could I, by taking this course, serve the cause of these women? There was only one way. I remembered your Majesty's unfaltering justice. My only hope was to appeal to that justice, not on my own behalf, but on theirs. While giving up my life for them, I might ask that you would yourself examine their story, and do justice between them and their enemy."

The voice sank towards the end of the story, until it was little more than a whisper. There was a brief pause, and then Mr. Herbertson added, in words that seemed to be wrung from him with spasms of agony:

"My life is not worth such a favour. . . . It would be too small a price to pay even for this interview. . . . But it is all that I have to give. And because your Majesty has consented to hear me, I have the courage to hope."

Mr. Herbertson ceased. He stood waiting, with his hands quivering upon the edge of the table. He could not believe that he had done this thing—that he had made the appeal. But his haggard face told the story.

Several moments passed. The silence was charged with unutterable emotion. Never once did the Emperor's eyes, pitiless in their coldness, leave the man's face. When he began to speak it was in measured accents that matched his look:

"Let me translate your story. The man of whom you speak owed a debt to the honour of our House. That debt was his life. Circumstances have moved you to consider, after many years of silence, whether you might attempt to pay that debt on his behalf. But before doing so you wish to make a bargain with me, the Head of the House. Is it not so?"

Was it so? Did it amount to exactly that? Mr. Herbertson scarcely recognised his own story, and yet he felt that this version could not be denied. It was the same story from another angle. And the calm, ruthless voice went on:

"But, sir, there are some things which you have forgotten. You forget them because the Honour of our House has a code which you cannot understand."

Mr. Herbertson shrank before that contempt.

He looked as guilty as he had done in the presence
of Count Brode.

"One thing is this," the Emperor continued.
"You have forgotten that honour is not a thing
that can be bought and sold. A man of honour
does not put his honour in pledge or set a price
upon it. It is always beyond price. Such is the
code of our House, and the Head of the House
can know no other."

Mr. Herbertson stood very still. The Emperor
rose from his chair, but he had a little more to say.
He said it with the same biting scorn:

"Then as to your attempt to bargain with me.
Can you not see what an outrage it is? A debt
has been left undischarged for over twenty years—
and now you try to use it as an asset with which to
make a bargain! It shall be paid—if I will promise
a certain thing!"

The voice rose to a note of harshness. Every
word was like a hammer-blow. Mr. Herbertson
held his ground, but he shrank and quivered. His
weakness provoked a deeper scorn from his accuser.

"No," said the Emperor. "I cannot make you
understand. If that was your motive it is impossible that you should understand. But that man's
debt stands apart from any question of the Hamars.
That life is owing in any case, and you cannot traffic
with it."

The harsh note grew more harsh, the last words
had a force of passion behind them, the keen eyes
flashed anger as well as scorn. There was no
questioning the finality of the utterance, even if
the speaker had not made a gesture of dismissal;
yet Mr. Herbertson, though dazed, struggled with

a sudden fierce protest. *If that was your motive.
. . .* But he saw that it had never been his motive.
He had never had his motives clearly analysed
before, but in this moment of agony it was done.
No, that had not been his motive!

But it was too late, even if he had had the power
to speak, and he knew that he had not the power.
He could only stammer a helpless question:

"Is this—is this my answer?"

The Emperor did not reply. There was no
answer, or the answer had already been given.
Still there was a moment left, and in that moment
Mr. Herbertson saw that one thing stood out clearly
in this maze of wretchedness and misunderstanding.

"The debt," he cried, "the debt shall be paid!
Your Majesty shall know when it is done. The
rest is in your hands. I will do all that I can do."

There was a note of passion, almost of defiance,
in his voice. He searched the Emperor's face with
anguished eyes, heedless of his own words, but
knowing well their meaning. Then he received a
sign which he could not disobey, and he accepted it
with the realisation that all was over.

"I thank your Majesty," he said, "for hearing
me."

Then he passed out into the sunshine, to take
uneven steps down the broad path by which he
had come. And all the way he felt upon him the
steady gaze of the man he had left. Perhaps this
was only imagination, but it was like a whip of
scorpions.

At the first turn in the path he found some one
waiting for him, pacing slowly to and fro. It
was the Chancellor, thoughtful and anxious, who

at once turned to accompany him. They walked
together towards the door, passed out beyond the
silent sentries, and so into the other garden.

Not a word was said until they reached the side
door of the white house, by which Mr. Herbertson
had entered less than an hour before. Apparently
the parting was to be immediate, and there was
good reason for this. Ronnefeldt wished to return
to his master.

At the last, however, there was a pause. Mr.
Herbertson had recovered himself sufficiently to
remember what was due to the man who had
assisted him.

"I am grateful for your Excellency's help," he
said earnestly.

The Chancellor seemed to turn while his hand
was upon the lock. He inclined his head in acknowledgment. Then, as if moved by a sudden
impulse of pity, he held out his hand to his pale
and shaken guest. But the amazing Mr. Herbertson did not take it. With some murmur of excuse
he shrank from it and then passed quickly out into
the street. He heard the door closed behind him.

The Chancellor lost no time in returning to the
garden, where he found his master still sitting in
the summer-house.

"He is gone?" asked the Emperor.

"Yes, sire."

The Chancellor looked at the old man with
anxious eyes. He saw that the Emperor's strength
had gone, his sternness with it.

"It was a strange thing," murmured the old
man. "Of course he will not do it. It is con-
stitutionally impossible to him. But there is the

idea, the aspiration. And that is something, Ronnefeldt."

"Yes, sire."

"It is a spark where one had not looked for it. Well, that is done with now, and we will leave it. There is no profit in it. . . . You have the outline of your Measure to show me. We will examine it here."

Silently the Chancellor took out a folded paper. He opened it and laid it down before the Emperor. It contained a number of suggestions neatly laid out under a series of headings. Quickly, briefly, with masterly lucidity, he gave the necessary explanations. The Emperor glanced down the list, heard all with strained, unfaltering attention, and then looked straight before him down the garden path. It was some time before he spoke.

"It is bold, and it reads well. You are conceding much, but you are asking for something. And they have been accustomed to give nothing. I have little hope that they will accept, though you have done much to prepare the way for it."

He shook his head. The Chancellor made no remark, and the silence continued for some minutes. Then the Emperor said:

"I fear that you are building to some extent on that man, Ronnefeldt. If so, you will be bitterly disappointed. There is no help there."

"No, sire, unless—"

"Ha! you are thinking of that factor. Your faith in it is pathetic! But even if it is present—which you do not know—it will never work that miracle."

Again there was silence. The Emperor understood it.

"You do not believe me? You think it possible?" he asked; and there was kindness in the
tones and in the look. This ruler knew that it
was his province to get the best out of all men,
those whom he loathed as well as those whom he
loved; but though this gave him a Brode as well
as a Ronnefeldt, he was in no danger of misplac-
ing his affections.

"Sire," said Ronnefeldt, "with that factor I believe all things possible—even this thing."

The Emperor folded the paper and returned it
to him. "You are still a young man, Ronnefeldt,"
he said, "and it is good for all of us that you are.
We will hope and work for the best. Now let us
go in."

He rose wearily, and they left the place together.

Chapter XIII

Mr. Herbertson Writes a Letter

AFTER the interview Mr. Herbertson made his way back to his hotel, and an hour later was being driven to the railway station. He could find time for thought during the journey. Besides, there was now no purpose to serve by remaining in this land of nightmare. He longed for the refuge of his garden.

When the time for thought came, it brought him anything but comfort. He saw that he had not obtained the assurance he had asked for, and again and again he burned with humiliation and shame. But he remembered, too, that although he had not obtained a pledge he had given one. He had come here to obtain a promise in return for a sacrifice. In the event, he had pledged himself to accomplish the sacrifice without obtaining the promise. The Salzburg honour was an inexorable code. Inexorable! Under the circumstances his confusion of mind was not surprising. He did not know whether he had failed in his mission, but he knew that he had not succeeded!

While he suffered the keenest shame, he blamed himself utterly for his folly in undertaking such a cause. He would abandon it now, and recommence life in some quarter of the world where he could

once more, and this time for ever, cut himself free
from old ties. This mood would pass, and he would
recall the more favourable signs. There was the
fact that he had been heard, there was the Chancellor's offer of his hand. Then there was the
pledge he had given. Honour he had considered
a thing apart from him; but— And then he thought
of the Emperor himself, so lonely, so pathetic a
figure, with his high standard of action and his
life of disappointment and tragedy. When to these
was added the thought of those who awaited his
return, he felt that only one course was possible
to him. His life was of no value to any one; here
was a chance—just a chance—of making it finally
useful. He would take that chance in that hope, but
he would take it even if there were no hope. What
better could he do with this last possession?

His journey was as long as it was wretched, for
he had had no heart to arrange his times; and
when he reached Waldington one day by some early
morning train, it was after practically a week of
sleepless travelling. But there was little time for
sleep now if he intended to send Count Brode his
answer before the term had expired. The great
question must be decided at once.

At the hour of his arrival the house was silent,
and he let himself in with his latchkey. He went
to his study, but there was something in that
familiar atmosphere that repelled him. Nor had
he any inclination for the garden, a fact which gave
him vague surprise. Were the old things losing
their charm for him, or was this troubled and
tempest-tossed spirit ill-prepared for their quiet
influences? Perhaps it was that he had not yet

thrown off the shadows of those other experiences through which he had passed—the great square of the cathedral, the Imperial gardens and the kingly old man who had walked in them. Surely, Gethsemane and the Garden of Illusion must always be alien to one another!

After a while he went to his dining-room, drew up the blind, and took a seat in the window: and when Mrs. Jenner came downstairs she found him dozing in his chair. One look at his haggard face confirmed all her forebodings.

"Good gracious!" she cried, in mingled astonishment and alarm. "Are you ill, sir? You look dreadful!"

"I have travelled rather too hurriedly," he explained, her anxiety putting him to shame at once. "But I think a little breakfast will soon put me right."

She vanished upon the word, with the unpleasant conviction that things were going from bad to worse; but she was placed upon her mettle, and in less than fifteen minutes had prepared a comfortable breakfast, to which the traveller was forced to apply himself. But directly he had satisfied his supposed hunger he returned to his chair and his problem; and Mrs. Jenner, a woman, as we have seen, not devoid of perception, retired to her kitchen to keep her questions and her sympathy for a more convenient season.

The next thing that called Mr. Herbertson out of his maze of hopeless reverie was a smart tap at the window. Hadfield was smiling at him from without. He was just starting for his office, and had chanced to see his neighbour in passing.

Mr. Herbertson opened the window. He tried to seem his old self. "So you're back," cried Hadfield. "Why, how ill you look!"

"Do I?" said Mr. Herbertson. "Mrs. Jenner says the same. Well, it has been rather a rush."

"Yes, I suppose so. But if I may ask, how did you get on?"

Mr. Herbertson hesitated. "Oh," he said, "fairly well, I think. But I'll tell you all about it later."

There was a pause. The young man was conscious of constraint, and the other could say little at the present juncture. It was not until now that he remembered the invalid next door—that is to say, remembered her consciously, though of course she had been in his thoughts through all these restless days. His forgetfulness filled him with compunction. He had not even enquired of Mrs. Jenner!

"How is the Countess?" he asked quickly. "I hope she continues to improve."

Then Hadfield beamed with satisfaction. "The Countess? She is making excellent progress. The doctor is delighted. I think it is chiefly due to you. She feels that somebody is doing something—that things are moving. Yesterday she got up at twelve o'clock, and stayed up for two hours. What do you think of that?"

"I am delighted to hear it. I will send Mrs. Jenner in with a message. It was a good thing you saw me. Good morning."

Hadfield went off in great good-humour, and Mr. Herbertson closed the window. To his relief he found that this brief talk had had a good effect upon him, and that he was able to look at things much more reasonably. There was always a very healthful atmosphere about Hadfield. Calling his housekeeper, he sent her in to Mrs. Hadfield's with a message for the Countess. He had travelled all night, he said, and would take two or three hours' rest; but if she would see him at noon, he would be glad to give her what news he had.

This duty accomplished, he went upstairs, and actually slept soundly until near the time he had mentioned. Home was asserting its claims at last. A bath assisted him further in the process of revival, and when he passed through the garden he discovered to his joy that the nightmare of the week was gradually being dissipated. Mrs. Hadfield came to greet him with outstretched hand, a touch of life and reality that was very gracious indeed, exclaimed at his somewhat worn appearance, and at once announced him. Then Rhona came to meet him on the stairs, her face flushed with pleasure. Better and better. He was a man again!

"We are so pleased," she said. "We were anxious for you, Mr. Herbertson."

"There was no need," he said gratefully. "I was not in danger for a single hour. It gives me pleasure to find the Countess better."

"She is much better," said the girl happily, and apparently much younger for her happiness. "Come."

The Countess was reclining in an invalid chair, and it was easy to see that she had made good progress during the days of her protector's ordeal. The wasted features had gained contour and repose, and there was a new serenity in those eyes which had learned to look for danger and misfortune in every movement that took place near her. She even made an attempt to rise, but he checked it quickly.

"No," he said, "do not move. I will sit near you to give you my news. You see that I have come back—and in safety."

"We are glad," said the Countess. "We were very anxious."

He gave some trifling account of his journey homewards, and congratulated her upon her restored health; and during these moments he discovered to his intense relief that his period of indecision was definitely over. Perhaps there was an atmosphere here which was capable of strengthening the faint heart and raising a man to his best levels. Indeed, there must be, for had he not experienced it before?

That was why he was able to tell the story he did. A few hours before he had not known what news to communicate, what results to disclose.

"Now," he said pleasantly, "you are waiting for my news. It is not final and definite, Countess, but there is still something good to tell you. I obtained an interview with the Chancellor."

Astonishment took the place of expectation. "Ronnefeldt?" murmured the Countess. "You saw Ronnefeldt?"

"I saw him. Before I left here I knew that he was at Graaden, and had resolved to try to see him. Perhaps I should explain, however, that it was not by any merit of my own that I succeeded. Years ago Adrian of Zell served the Chancellor to good purpose, and I knew of the incident. I did not hesitate to use it; and it was for that sake that the Baron consented to hear me."

They were a little bewildered by this development. The relations between the unfortunate strangers and their protector had been of a somewhat complex and indefinite nature owing to the peculiar circumstances; but Mr. Herbertson had always exhibited a deference which showed that he did not forget the place from which they had fallen. Now, after a pause, the Countess looked at him with an entirely new regard. It could not be expressed in words, but adjustments had been made.

"And the result?" she asked eagerly. "Oh, he is a man, the Chancellor. I have met him only twice, but I felt that I could trust him."

"You are right, Countess," answered Mr. Herbertson. "Baron Ronnefeldt is a man to be trusted, a man whose integrity is equal to his ability. He acknowledged the claim upon his attention, though the man is dead to whom his debt was due. Finally I obtained this concession: that all the circumstances of your case should be laid before the Emperor, with an urgent appeal for revision."

Still looking into his face, the Countess opened her lips to speak. But the flush died away from her cheeks, and her head sank back upon the cushions. Rhona moved to her side, but she recovered at once. Even the weakest may bear the shock of joy!

"Ah," she said, "the news overcomes me. It is so good! You have reached the fountain-head! It is far beyond all that I dared to hope, though I knew that you would do your utmost. I had almost begun to fear—indeed, I have sometimes dreamed it—that we should never see Lusia again, never see our home at Cronia. Can you imagine the horror of such a nightmare? I can trust the Emperor—when he knows the truth."

"He cannot but know it now," said Mr. Herbertson. "Moreover, my visit would remind the Chancellor—perhaps he had forgotten it before—that the first fault lay, not with Count Mathias but with the man who influenced him. It shall not be obscured again, and it must have weight."

There was a pause. They did not necessarily follow his reasoning, but were content to hear his views without question. And having expressed this view, he came back to the immediate moment.

"But I must ask you, Countess, to be patient, and not to expect news too soon. Kings and Governments move very deliberately. What they do, they do slowly; what they undo, they do more slowly still."

"Patience is easy when there is hope," said the Countess, gratefully. "You shall never see a question in my eyes, Mr. Herbertson."

"We will not forget," said Rhona, with a smile. "We will let a month pass without a word."

"Very good. That is a reasonable time. In the meantime I may have to go to the Continent again—to confirm my evidence. But you will leave the rest to me."

He rose with those confident words, and thus brought the interview to an end. All through he had dominated it, not on account of his news, but largely by the assurance of his manner. The Countess realised some difference in him, but could not identify it. She was to consider it when he had gone and to give her conclusion at a later date.

"You are going so soon?" she protested. "You have not given us time to thank you."

There was no sign of uncertainty in the man's answer. "Thank me when all is done," he said, smiling. "This morning I have to write a letter. Good-bye."

In that mood he left her, Rhona accompanying him down the stairs. But he scarcely spoke until they parted at the door of Mrs. Hadfield's dining-room, and even then it was only a brief farewell.

"Good—very good," he said. "I am so glad!"

She could not answer that except by a look of gratitude. He did not take the gratitude to himself, for he was not thinking of himself at all. There was an exaltation in her presence, but it only thrilled him now with the thought that the deed of her release was drawn. And he felt that he could put his signature to it.

He walked down the garden to reach his own grounds with a light step but with an absent look; and he did not once glance back to observe that the girl was following him with eyes of gravity and bewilderment. Yet he did not write his letter at once. Instead, he took the round of his garden, glancing at every well-known feature as he passed —the box borders which he had set and tended as if they were the most important matters in life, the fruit-trees he had selected and planted with his own hands, the rose-beds with their many choice bushes each of which he knew by name. And all of them were astir with life, greater, richer life than on that day of his call, the Second of May.

"In a month," he said, half aloud, "the garden will be in full bloom. And I—where shall I be?

Gone down to death, undoubtedly. And yet, though I shall be dead then, I cannot feel that I am dying now. I rather feel that I am only just beginning to live. I am about a month old, for my birthday was the Second of May; but I am not a child of a month, but a man of a month." .

This was reflection quite in his old manner, and he capped it by another equally whimsical:

"It is curious, though, that I cannot reach full stature unless I die. It is a process of growth that will find its completion very suddenly by a pistol-shot or the passage of a rapier."

Then he paused before his garden greenhouse —that gaunt skeleton of brick and timbers which now seemed destined never to be completed. He surveyed the chaos with another quaint suggestion:

"She mistook you for a Ruin," he said. "And you are a Building. Let us hope that Count Brode has made the same mistake with regard to your master. . . . And now, to add another brick, let us go and write that letter."

Chapter XIV

Mr. Herbertson Comes Out of a Tunnel

"GOOD gracious, Mr. Herbertson! You are gardening in your next-to-best suit."

Mr. Herbertson looked up from his tunnel, the tunnel which had been the doom of the man from Doveton's. Margaret Joan stood above him on the verge, bareheaded, her expressive face full of shocked wonder.

"And you have one of your best shirts on, too," she added. "Oh, this is too much! Did you forget?"

Mr. Herbertson, leaning on his spade, shook his head. "No," he said, "I didn't. It was purposely done."

"But why? What wonderful thing has happened?"

"Ah, that's just the word, Margaret Joan. It was what people used to call a vision. I actually thought I saw a goddess in the garden."

"A goddess?" said Margaret gravely. "Actually?" And her gravity was immediately illumined by the light of mischief. "Let's guess how. She saw this greenhouse from a long distance, and thought it was a church. Because of those chapel windows. But when she came up close she was

184

filled with conclusion—no, confusion. Which, Mr. Herbertson?"

"Both, perhaps," said the man in the next-to-best suit. "Anyway, she thought it was a ruin. So I've had to start work on it again. And as she may return, I've had to change my clothes. So now you know."

"Yes," agreed Margaret Joan. "And if you ask me, Mr. Herbertson, I think it was high time. But what are you going to do with the old ones?"

"Oh, I don't know. I haven't thought of that."

"I have," said Margaret. "But I hesitate to mention it. I've often wanted to, but mamma thought you might be annoyed."

"You can trust me not to be annoyed, I hope?"

"Most certainly, Mr. Herbertson. I have lots of faith in you. Well, if you really don't want that old suit any longer, why not let me and Phyllis have it? For the Fifth of November."

"Well, upon my word!" said the astonished Mr. Herbertson; and Margaret hastened to apply what balm she might.

"It's no re-flection on you," she said earnestly. "It's only that it's the oldest suit of clothes about here. And if you kept it in the house, you know, you might forget, and put it on again."

"Yes. I might fall from grace. Well, I accept the explanation. The suit is yours. I will instruct Mrs. Jenner to hand it over to you in due course."

"Now isn't that gorgeous!" cried Margaret, gleefully. "And wasn't it lucky that I came to-day, soon after the goddess? In the tick of time, as daddy says."

Mr. Herbertson did not think it necessary to correct that expression. He climbed out of his tunnel by a short flight of steps which had once led to the upper deck of one of the Waldington tramcars. It was thus that he collected the materials for his work as occasion offered, with a quite catholic freedom and a very considerable gift of adaptability. The result was that while he had found surprisingly happy use for many articles cheaply obtained, there was something that suggested a museum in the extraordinary collection of odds and ends to be found in his greenhouse. Reaching the level earth, he took a seat on a wooden bench which, like the windows, had come from the old chapel of the Primitive Methodists. Then he drew Margaret Joan to his side. She came quite confidently, but with expectation in her eyes. Mr. Herbertson was different from every other man she knew, and provided a surprise very frequently.

He took her hand to draw her nearer. Margaret Joan's hand had been busy with the world's work for some time, but it had not lost its dimpled softness. Herbertson had often admired it before, but now the wonder and beauty of that exquisite little instrument found a link with something already in his mind. "The eccentric Providence which turns these out by the million with sublime unconcern— what a standard it must have!" And for a moment he could not look up into the child's face to meet the greater marvel of her eyes. But Margaret Joan gave a sigh of relief. She had stolen a glance at her finger-nails.

"No," he said. "They're not so bad to-day."

She sighed again and laughed. They understood each other so well.

"They're such a bother!" she said.

"Yes. Such a standard is a bit of a bother. But we feel very uncomfortable if we don't work up to it."

"*I* don't!" said Margaret Joan, unashamed.

"No. Not yet."

He raised the hand to his lips. "There!" she cried. "I knew you would do something. You really are the limit!" And she nestled closer, partly in admiration, partly in compassion.

"But since I am older," said Mr. Herbertson, "I have to work up to it as far as I can. And I am sorry to say, Margaret Joan, that I shall not be able to come to your Birthday Party."

"Oh, you don't mean that. You *promised!*" cried Margaret, wide-eyed in protest.

"It is true. I did. Indeed, I have been looking forward to your birthday for months and months. But I find that I have to go away again for a fortnight or so, and that will be one of the weeks."

There was a long pause, full of dismay. Then:— "When I woke up this morning," said Margaret Joan, "I never dreamed that I should get such bad news as this. But isn't there some way out of it? We could have the party later."

This was an enormous concession. But Mr. Herbertson felt very sure that he would not be able to attend even then! He shook his head.

"It would be awful to have to postpone it," he said. "Think of the extra days' waiting!"

"Oh, but I know. We could have it earlier. We could have it before you go."

"That would almost be worse. It would be all over and done with, ever so long before it should be. And when the real birthday came you would be filled with sorrow and regret."

"But I'd get my presents sooner."

"You might. But some people would get muddled, and forget to send them at all. I have another plan."

"I might have guessed that you had," said Margaret. "You always have. What is it—quick?"

"Well, I propose this. I propose that instead of having me, you invite the young lady who is visiting Mr. Hadfield—Miss Franks."

Margaret's face lit up. She had seen Rhona several times, and worshipped her with all the quick, eager admiration of a child's heart. In the emotion of the moment she spoke as she felt —at the moment.

"Oh," she sighed, "that would be glorious! That would be ever so better!"

Ever so better! Mr. Herbertson did not appear to notice the remark. No one could have guessed that the little tongue had stabbed him mightily.

"She *will* be glorious," he said heartily: "I can promise you that. To tell the truth, Margaret Joan, I rather fancy she had something to do with the goddess I thought I saw the other day."

"Of course," said Margaret Joan. "I guessed at the very beginning. You often forget that I'm almost grown-up. . . . But now I must go and tell mamma and Phyllis about the clothes. Shall I tell Mrs. Jenner, too, in case you forget?"

"It might be advisable. My memory is shockingly unsafe. Tell her as you go through the house."

The child, with a swift and happy "Good-bye," followed by a kiss that was as free from consciousness as it was perfect in heartiness, made for the house with all the speed of exuberant life and health. A moment, and she had passed out of sight to astonish Mrs. Jenner.

Mr. Herbertson remained on his Primitive Methodist bench and sought a cigarette. As he smoked it his first reflection dealt with his own folly in being so easily wounded. "Why will you continue to expect so much from other people?" he mused. "And a child, too! Have you given other people so much that you may justly demand so much? And you cannot keep a fair balance-sheet. That child has given you incalculable pleasure. For two years she has been light and gladness in your unprofitable existence. She prays for you every evening of her life, and often dreams of you, though you are not worthy to sweep the road before her. Yet you allow your black heart to be wounded by just one little slip of her baby tongue, the impulse of an instinctive admiration as pure as a snowdrop. You be hanged for a skunk!"

He paused to allow the lecture to sink in. Then he continued:

"You won't be hanged. You are going to be shot. Let us refresh your memory with the geography of it."

From his vest pocket he took a folded slip of paper, the contents of an envelope which had arrived by the midday post. There was no address at the head of the slip, and it was also unsigned, but it was a model of lucid and definite instruction:

"Saint Claud is a small fishing village and watering place near Tréport. There is one hotel, the Seine, where you will find us at any time during next week. Everything can be arranged there. Ask for Herr Pasberg, of Cologne."

"There!" said Mr. Herbertson. "Everything nicely on the way, with a minimum of trouble, expense and delay. There is an excellent Master of the Ceremonies in charge, to see that nothing goes wrong; and I'm pretty sure that nothing will go wrong unless you go wrong. And that, James, is just the trouble. No one who knew you could depend upon you to turn up at this little fishing village and watering-place. . . . And if you did turn up, who would dare to say that you would stay there? The odds are all against it."

The cigarette was finished. Mechanically he sought another, but suddenly stayed his hand.

"No," he said. "You must not. Your first duty at the present moment is an apology to Margaret Joan. When you have finished her Birthday Present your contrite heart may be a little easier. So you'll get down to it instanter."

He rose, put away his spade, and went up towards the house. As he passed along the dividing wall he saw that the French doors of Hadfield's sitting-room were open, and that the Countess and Rhona were sitting there in the sun. The mother sat in an easy basket-chair, and the girl on a pouffe at her feet. They saw Mr. Herbertson over the wall as he approached, and Rhona rose.

"This is the happiest thing I have seen for a long time," he said. "Countess, I congratulate you."

The Countess smiled in reply. "You are very good, Mr. Herbertson. Yes, but I have had excellent nurses—and a very helpful neighbour."

"It is only the first time to be out here," said Rhona. "She shall sit in the sun for ten minutes to-day, and to-morrow it shall be twenty minutes. That is the direction of Dr. Henslow."

"May his shadow never grow less!" said Mr. Herbertson. "And it is very important that all should go well, for there is a Function shortly at Number Fourteen. I have promised that you shall take my place at Margaret Joan's birthday, and she has been graciously pleased to accept the change."

He explained the characteristics of such a festival, details which Rhona comprehended without difficulty and received with such earnest attention that she forgot to enquire the cause of his own inability to be present. Once again Mr. Herbertson noticed the stars in her eyes (surely, only a futile and old-fashioned person would have done this!) and presently discovered that those lights were causing him some aberration of thought and a little confusion of speech. It was excusable, he reflected afterwards, for he had never noticed that precise effect in human eyes before, and every Wise Man will follow a New Star. But the discovery occurred before the excuse, and when he made it he blamed himself for boorishness, and brought the talk to an end. Rhona returned to her seat and he passed on to his study.

"He is very kind," murmured the Countess, "and very simple-hearted."

There was a pause. "Is it not strange to find

such a man in such a place?" said the girl at last.

The Countess hesitated before she replied. Then she spoke slowly with obvious reserve.

"Sometimes, child, men hide themselves because they have something to conceal."

Rhona started. "Mother! Not that—with this man! You cannot mean it?"

"I do not mean it with this man," said the mother gently. "And even if it were something to conceal it need not be a crime. But it is wise, dearest one, to try to see things as they are, while hoping and believing the best."

Rhona did not look into her mother's face. She was gazing down the garden, beyond Hadfield's farther wall to the timbers of Mr. Herbertson's egregious greenhouse showing through the foliage of his cherry trees. Her mother touched her cheek affectionately. During these last months of agony her child had become a woman. She was concerned for the happiness of this child-woman, yet she could not speak plainly.

"And after all," she said, "I have never met a man of whom it was easier to hope and believe good things. And now, I think, my time out here is ended. Is it not so?"

Meanwhile Mr. Herbertson, having cleaned from his hands the marks of the garden, had settled down at his desk. Before him lay the water-colour drawing intended for Margaret Joan's birthday, and now almost completed. It showed a very formidable castle fortress, set upon a rocky eminence with forest-clad hills looming behind. A zig-zag road, with frequent barriers of massive gates, led to the main entrance, which was heavily guarded by buttressed towers: and each corner of the building also had its tower, duly battlemented. Originally these had been of a species unfamiliar to Western eyes, but on consideration the artist had replaced his first designs by structures of Norman type. There was a suggestion of a park in the foreground, and a broad stream aggressively blue.

"Yes," mused Mr. Herbertson, critically. "I think it should do. That river is so blue that it might suggest the Blue Danube. But those Norman towers—there is no such architecture on the Blue Danube!"

Another thought came: "A strong place, with strength and power all about it. A man bred in such a hold as this might be expected to breathe into his being something of that power and restraint. . . . Perhaps the fault was that he left it too soon—at fifteen or so, I believe. Then the fever and folly and fret of the Court, heady and maddening. No, Adrian, I am sure it would have been better had you stayed at home for at least a little longer. But there was no one to see to it."

The drawing was to be enclosed in a dainty leather-bound case, with Margaret's initials on the side, and a letter which Mr. Herbertson had written was to face the drawing. He now spent an absorbed hour in transcribing this letter, for it must have an initial in red, and a tailpiece ornament drawn with absurd care. That was in the original plan, but now he added extra care, the fruit of self-reproach. Having completed this task he laid the unusual gift away in his desk just as Mrs. Jenner called him. "And now," he said to himself, "you may feel a little better, having atoned by much

labour of the hands for that slip of the heart. And
so to tea."

During tea he planned the next step. Before
Margaret had called him out of his tunnel he had
fought his way through much earth and much
doubt and uncertainty. The noon post had brought
the call to make yet one more stage on the road
of doom, and it had not been an easy matter to
take that stage. It was not the final stage, and
it was largely his distrust of his power to continue
to the end that made this next stage so doubtful.

He could not believe that it was possible for him
to fight the fight through. No one believed that
he would do it, not Brode nor Ronnefeldt, nor the
Emperor—nor himself. All were of one mind in
this matter. Then why not abandon the folly now,
rather than delay the certain fiasco for another
week or two? So through a tense hour he had
fought the old, unending battle, the battle that he
fought in craven dreams and in those deadly hours
when sleep refused to come and all the spectres
of fear and shame gathered round his bed. A
dozen times he lost, and began the fight again,
impelled by self-scorn, and lured, perhaps, by the
hope that is a last spark even in the feeblest heart.

Then Margaret had come, with her clear, pure
eyes and the affection that had no doubt in it.
When he had taken her hand the legions of vacilla-
tion had retired, and he had fixed his course; then
he had seen Rhona and the Countess, and he
wondered that the fight had been so hard. Why,
no other course was possible! And now—

"And now, James," he said grimly, "since you
need so much of spur and persuasion, we must

find means to keep you to the steep path of—well, of honour. Wherefore the next interview must be with Mr. Hadfield."

It took place an hour or two later, and was a very interesting interview for George. "Hadfield, old man," cried his neighbour, over that helpful wall, "have you done anything about your holiday yet?"

"Not a thing," said Hadfield. "It's all in abeyance. We had been thinking of going away somewhere for a week or two, but nothing had been fixed. And now that we have our guests, you see—"

"Of course," said Mr. Herbertson. "Just as I thought. You cannot both go while they are with you. But could you have gone whenever you pleased, as far as your office is concerned?"

"Why, yes, except for August. The Heads and the seniors reserve August, usually. One of the perquisites of infirmity."

"Just so. Well, now, could you go quite promptly if you wished? Could you go, say, on Monday?"

"On Monday?"

"Yes. The very next Monday that is. It is here that I come in, you see, like a Providence— a rather eccentric Providence, perhaps—to try to arrange your holiday for you. I have to go to the Continent on Monday on that little business, and it would be an ideal thing if you could join me. . . . Would you like it?"

"Like it?" echoed Hadfield. "Rather!"

"And could you get off, do you think?"

"I haven't the slightest doubt about that. I have a few days to get things ready. In fact I can say definitely that there is no question about it."

"Then we'll consider it settled. That's really A.1. It will be a delight to have your company. We'll take up our quarters at a little seaside place from which we can make excursions frequently, and by the time my little affair is over, you'll have seen quite a lot of France. But come down the garden, and I'll tell you all about it."

They walked down, the wall between them, Mr. Herbertson looking so pleased that no one could have guessed his revolt against this necessary legion of lies. "But that's another thing that will be over soon," he thought. "One of the compensations of the end." And a moment later, seated once more on the Primitive Methodist bench, he shared his useful cigarettes and revealed his plans.

"I brought you down here," he explained, "because I did not wish to be overheard. A certain part of this business must be classed as 'confidential' for the present. It would be alarming because it would be misunderstood. The fact is, old fellow, that the company of a friend is very necessary, because this is not altogether a picnic. I am booked to fight a duel."

Hadfield's incredulity was sufficiently complete. "What! A duel? You?"

"Just that. Pistols for two and coffee for four, you know. And as there must be four to drink the coffee, I must have a second."

It was difficult to take him seriously, but Hadfield knew his neighbour sufficiently well to see that there might be a fact behind that frivolous manner. He reached it by a very simple bit of reasoning.

"By Jove!" he said. "That young Brode!"

"Why, you have it," cried Mr. Herbertson.

"You see, Hadfield, things on the Continent are not as they are here. Apart from the silly political duels in France, the most ordinary cause of a duel is, of course, a dispute about a woman. One aspect of my interference in the Brode-Hamar affair amounts to this—that I have placed myself between this fiery young man and the lady he wishes to secure. Consequently, by the custom in Styria, he is entitled to challenge me."

"But you have appealed," said Hadfield.

"Quite so. But my appeal to the Chancellor concerns the restoration of the ladies to their home. My affair with young Philip is a thing apart, though not altogether apart. Since I have intervened in his somewhat peculiar courtship he is entitled to 'call me out,' and if I can give him what is called 'satisfaction' in this way, the whole business will be neatly rounded off. I shall have complied with a national custom of which I cannot profess ignorance, and he will be able to hold up his head because he has punished my interference in the only way a fire-eating Styrian officer can recognise. Is it clear now?"

It was not quite clear. "Punished?" said Hadfield. "Then it's risky?"

"Risky? My dear fellow, have you ever heard of a modern duel that ended fatally?"

Hadfield could not remember one.

"Oh," he said. "Then it's to be a mere matter of form?"

"It's to be a mere matter of form. Honour will be satisfied as long as two shots are fired, wherever the bullets go, and whether there are any bullets or not. Philip will save his face, and the great Styrian Army will have vindicated its honour. . . . And can you imagine, Hadfield, that the Brodes would be likely to get themselves into three kinds of trouble by killing a British subject, with a Styrian army revolver, perhaps, on French soil?"

"I should say they were not such asses as that."

"They are not, by any means. I haven't the slightest doubt as to the result of this encounter. And now that you are satisfied as to my safety, I will give you the details."

He produced the letter and sketched his proposal for the journey. Starting early on the Monday morning, they would spend one night in Paris and get down to Saint Claud on the Tuesday. "We'll have that pleasant little holiday and satisfy this gallant gentleman without trouble and with expedition," he explained. "We'll kill several birds with one stone. But, of course, the women must not know all the particulars. They will assume that we are going to Styria, and we must leave them under that impression."

"Of course," said Hadfield. "They wouldn't understand."

"Then that is settled?"

"Decidedly, as far as I am concerned."

"You are a brick. Then I'll accept the invitation to-day, and you can tell your wife. I'll go in and tell the Countess in the morning. She must be tired this evening. She has been out in the garden for the first time."

So Mr. Herbertson arranged the whole programme, having a very plain, unsuspicious young man with whom to deal; and Hadfield was so charmed that he had no room for searching questions. His wife was equally charmed when he told her, and as he was unable to tell her all, she had no reason for suspicion. Had she known all the details her keen wit might have discovered more than one weak spot in that handsome fabric of deception. '. . .

Meanwhile Philip Brode had gone back for the present to Paris, where he spent most of his time. The birds were in the net and could not escape, so there was no reason why he should not make life as interesting as possible while he waited. So in Paris he loved much, as he understood love, and played much, and drank considerably; and he sometimes paused to give a thought to the rendezvous at Saint Claud. Then his face darkened, until it became the face of a devil. For the thought of Saint Claud was a probe into a raw wound that would never cease to smart as long as memory performed its natural function.

That epithet, Mr. Herbertson, was surely a great mistake.

Chapter XV

The Garden Is Blotted Out, and There Are No Stars

MARJORIE HADFIELD was an extremely happy young matron. Life had been sufficiently interesting before, but now her cup seemed to overflow. The home of which she was proud with a young housewife's pride had received guests of honour whose care was her delight and whose presence was an unfailing fount of satisfaction. Moreover, Mr. Herbertson had insisted that she must have a maid, for the time at least, and a willing little girl had been added to the household to be a crown of joy. In those days Mrs. Hadfield's life was a happy dream marvellously full of business.

This was the lady who greeted Mr. Herbertson next morning, when he went in to see the Countess. Entering, by arrangement, from the garden, he was led into the kitchen, where she was making cake. As a cake-maker she made an exceedingly attractive picture, and the visitor renewed his pleasure in that dark, vivid, girlish face and its piquant, challenging expression. Her vivacity was always such a delightful contrast to the boyish stolidity of her husband.

"So you are taking my husband away?" she said; and Mr. Herbertson, leaning against the edge of the table, admitted the charge.

"Yes, madam. And it is very good of you to let him go."

"He needs a holiday."

"So do you, no doubt."

"No. I am having one now. Every hour of the day."

Mr. Herbertson understood, and was pleased. He noticed that Mrs. Hadfield still wore the nameless garment which had attracted his attention on the Second of May, and that it suited her equally well with the sleeves turned back to the elbows. Floury hands were not unattractive, and it was possible to display a considerable amount of grace in the manipulation of a rolling-pin. There might be the germ of an essay in this discovery. He would make a note of it when he returned to his study. Then he raised his eyes from the floury hands to meet a smile vivid in its nature and tonic in its effect. But was "vivid" the best word for the nature of that smile? He must consider this again. Meanwhile, under the tonic influence of that same smile, he proceeded to his business.

"Is the Countess ready to see me?"

"She is waiting, Mr. Herbertson. Just go in."

Mr. Herbertson went.

Mrs. Hadfield heard him go in. She proceeded with her cake-making, but her mind was with Mr. Herbertson. The problem had become much more interesting of late: and now, quite suddenly, it assumed a new aspect. How old was Mr. Herbertson? He sometimes looked forty-five or even less, but there were times when he seemed much older. He was deferential to every one, but there was some special quality in his attitude to the Countess. She was slowly growing stronger, and in good health would be a comely and noble woman. Mr. Herbertson was a gentleman and a scholar: what if his great services should have a wonderful result, in, say, twelve months' time! . . . Mrs. Hadfield's eyes glowed again. What a sensation for Waldington! *On Wednesday, at Westminster Abbey, by the Right Rev. the Lord Bishop of London, James Herbertson, Esq., of Waldington, to the Countess Hamar. Among the guests were—*

Then Mrs. Hadfield laughed aloud, very prettily. Reflecting a little further, she was not quite satisfied. Mr. Herbertson looked positively young at times— and the Countess already had silver in her hair. An ideal match for him from the point of view of age would be some one just a few years younger. Even if she were ten years younger it would not be too much . . . or even fifteen. She was herself about fifteen years younger!—But at this point Mrs. Hadfield laughed again, and blushed, and decided that she would get George something very nice for his supper to-night. He was such a dear fellow . . . and he was little more than her own age.

The Countess had been trying to read the paper, but had found it sadly lacking in any point of contact for her. Naturally, Yesterday and To-morrow were her life, and to-day was but an interlude. As her face lit up Mr. Herbertson realised that she had made great progress even during the last few days.

"Then you have heard something?" she asked

eagerly. "Mr. Hadfield told us that you would bring news."

"It is not great news—it is nothing definite," said Herbertson quickly. "As I expected, I have been summoned to the Continent to give confirmation of my previous statement. Perhaps that is the simplest way of stating the fact. I have decided to go on Monday, and I have asked Mr. Hadfield to accompany me."

"But the news is good?" she pleaded. "Things are going well?"

"Things are going well. I spoke guardedly, but we have every reason to feel confident."

Rhona looked up into his face. "I think we understand," she said. "That is the truest kindness."

"And I hasten to say that our faith and trust are absolute," added the Countess, warmly. "But I hope you were aware of that before I spoke the words."

Mr. Herbertson realised that he had been aware of it, and flushed at the realisation. Perhaps humility was one of his besetting virtues.

"I am very grateful," he said. "Yes, I think I may say that things are going well. Indeed, I have some hope that this one journey may be enough."

"Ah," said the Countess, "if that is so, we may soon be in a position to repay some of our debt. You have done so much for us, and for no other reason than that you knew my husband long ago. It is a small cause for such great services."

Mr. Herbertson was so honest that he felt bound to explain: "Countess," he said, in a low tone, "let me say now that your view is too generous. I wish you to remember always that I am doing the plain man's duty of trying to right a wrong. I must try by all means to restore to you the happiness of which the folly of my master, Prince Adrian, deprived you. That is my purpose."

There was a long silence. The situation had never been clearly stated before, though there had been some consciousness of it. The Countess was touched, and met his look with a new sympathy.

"Oh," she said, "but you must not say that! You are not responsible for another man. Are you doing it because—because you once loved him? Is it that you would clear his name as far as you can?"

There was a long silence. "It may be that," was the grave answer. "There is no doubt that I once loved him. After that I despised him, and then I tried to forget him. Yet there is one thing I should like you to remember when these troubles are over and you are once again in your home."

"I shall remember many things," she answered. "But what is this one thing?"

"It is this. But for the power of Prince Adrian's name, I should never have gained the ear of the Chancellor. If your misfortunes are due to him, it may also be admitted that our present hope springs from the same source."

"It is strange," she said musingly. "But it is true."

"Strange and true. And if we succeed I trust that this strange truth will not be forgotten. There is so much on the debit side."

The Countess often found herself a little perplexed when Mr. Herbertson mentioned his quondam master. He always spoke with bitterness and contempt, yet she invariably got the impression that other and very different emotions might lie behind. To-day his bitterness was sufficiently pronounced, even while he admitted affection and pleaded that something might be remembered in the Prince's favour. She imagined that while he contemned the subject of their conversation he would have resented, though perhaps in silence, an attack from outside. This curious loyalty, once realised, moved her admiration as well as her compassion and she gave it a generous reward.

"Mr. Herbertson," she said gently, "I have never said a word against Prince Adrian. I never saw him, and I do not even know the whole story. But I do not blame him for our misfortunes. Mathias was older than he, and was himself responsible for the course he followed. Hear me, now, and believe me! I should no more think of blaming Prince Adrian than I should think of blaming you."

Mr. Herbertson looked considerably surprised. Perhaps the whole course of his own thoughts for many days had for the first time received a check.

"You are too charitable," he murmured.

"No, I am not charitable. I am only trying to be just. And now I will try to be grateful also, Mr. Herbertson, as I must be if I claim to have a heart. If the Prince had indeed been solely responsible for our misfortunes, as you have suggested, I should still refuse a word of blame against him. Your goodness would have wiped out everything, and would have raised a heavy debt on the other side."

Mr. Herbertson was moved by the warmth and

earnestness of that declaration. For a moment he looked into her eyes, a little bewildered, a little incredulous; then his face flushed hotly, and he turned his eyes away. He could not find words for the occasion, and the Countess smiled kindly at his confusion.

"Now I have spoken plainly," she said, "so plainly that the question is settled for ever, whether you succeed or not in your present mission.—And now let us speak of something else. I am glad that you are taking this young man with you. He is so to be trusted! And his little wife—what a heart of kindness she has shown us! Do you know what we shall do? When we go back we shall ask them to come and stay with us a while at Cronia. They shall see that we can be grateful."

Mr. Herbertson smiled. "You could not do anything that would please them more," he said; and at the mental picture of Hadfield's visit to Cronia he smiled again. There was no unkindness in the smile.

The days of that week passed swiftly, and he lived them fully. Strangely enough he was sometimes able to forget the end to which he was speeding; besides, he did his best to fill them with labour, so that there might be no void places where the spectres might enter. He completed another essay, he paid one or two visits to a solicitor, so that the *Finis* so soon to be written might be neat and clear, and he spent certain appointed hours of the day in his garden, keeping matters in order as far as was necessary. But he did not spend any of that precious time upon his greenhouse, for that amazing problem must be left for his successor.

He naturally saw much of the Hamars. Each day saw the Countess able to remain a little longer out of doors, and all those days were long, cloudless days when everything was speeding towards the consummation of summer. She found his company a very helpful thing, for he knew her own land sufficiently well to make a good listener when she spoke of it. He did not speak much of it himself, but she needed a listener rather than a conversationalist; and always there was that sympathetic manner, happily adapted to the circumstances. But if he gave much in those interviews he certainly received much, for he never went away to be tormented by doubt and indecision. In her presence the amazing thing that he had resolved to do seemed the only thing possible.

Perhaps, however, Rhona had the larger share in this effect, larger than he knew and utterly inconceivable to herself. As her mother recovered strength the daughter cast off the cloud of anxiety and allowed the natural beauty of a magnificent girlhood to come into the sunlight. One day Herbertson, at his desk, heard her singing in the garden, and paused to listen to a music which he had never heard before. When he realised whose voice it was he experienced a thrill of vivid pleasure, and remembered that morning of the Second of May when he had come out so unawares to breathe the glory of Spring. There was a link between these two experiences, but he thought that his pleasure arose from the reflection that but for him she would not have had the heart to sing. It would have been impossible in Franklyn Crescent.

Her attitude to him was frankly friendly, his

was that of an elder friend and protector who could occasionally be very light-hearted. His greenhouse was a kind of playground for them, and they spent a pleasant hour one afternoon in stocking it with dream-plants, from the imaginary top shelf to the chamber below. But as he could never forget the day of her first coming to the garden, he would always look for the gold in her hair, and, having found it, would look for the stars in her eyes. They were always there, but as they had a very disturbing effect upon his conversation an occasional glimpse must be enough.

The last day, the Sunday, was full of pleasant things, some of them happily planned and others happily unexpected. He went to morning service at St. Augustine's with Margaret Joan, but this time Rhona made a third in the party. She felt that it was safe to leave her mother for a short time, and Mr. Herbertson had suggested the adventure with one thought for Margaret's pleasure and one for his own. Margaret was certainly pleased, and during the service sat between the two, with a hand for each. As for him, the third member of the party was a source of great interest. This was Rhona's first experience of a Church service in England, except for visits to the Abbey and St. Paul's in earlier girlhood. She was intensely interested, not only in the service and the music, but in the worshippers around her. He supposed that it was as a subject for study that she gave him so keen a pleasure; but there was also some proprietary interest, he decided when he began to analyse that sentiment in his inevitable fashion. It seemed to him that she sat like a young and gravely curious Diana, glowing and beautiful, among those ordinary folk of this quiet old town. And but for him she would not have been there.

These elements would have been enough to make the service a new experience, but there were others that helped. The place of Margaret's favourite preacher was filled to-day by the Rector, so that instead of a raw youth attacking a formidable mystery, they heard an old man of much wisdom deal humbly and reverently with a simple and comforting thought—"The Shadow of the Almighty." This discourse was valuable for the experience that lay behind it, and beautiful for its humility; and Herbertson observed with interest that its hearers appeared to be listeners. This led him to certain reflections upon the Church's amazing neglect of her opportunities; but he did not see any personal application in the sermon, or in Margaret Joan's comment upon it when they had left the church.

"I expect it's a very big Shadow," she said.

When they reached home they met Dr. Henslow, leaving after his visit to his patient. He was in a very pleasant mood.

"Your mother is doing well, Miss Franks," he said. "I have granted her permission to have tea in the garden if she is careful not to stay out too long. I am sure that I can leave that to you."

"I also am sure," said Rhona. "It shall be a very happy day, and we will not spoil it." And with that she went in, leaving the young doctor warmed by some glow that might have come from the presence of a goddess. But he was a practical man, and only said to himself: "That girl is magnificent." Then he turned to Mr. Herbertson.

was that of an elder friend and protector who could occasionally be very light-hearted. His green-house was a kind of playground for them, and they spent a pleasant hour one afternoon in stocking it with dream-plants, from the imaginary top shelf to the chamber below. But as he could never forget the day of her first coming to the garden, he would always look for the gold in her hair, and, having found it, would look for the stars in her eyes. They were always there, but as they had a very disturbing effect upon his conversation an occasional glimpse must be enough.

The last day, the Sunday, was full of pleasant things, some of them happily planned and others happily unexpected. He went to morning service at St. Augustine's with Margaret Joan, but this time Rhona made a third in the party. She felt that it was safe to leave her mother for a short time, and Mr. Herbertson had suggested the adventure with one thought for Margaret's pleasure and one for his own. Margaret was certainly pleased, and during the service sat between the two, with a hand for each. As for him, the third member of the party was a source of great interest. This was Rhona's first experience of a Church service in England, except for visits to the Abbey and St. Paul's in earlier girlhood. She was intensely interested, not only in the service and the music, but in the worshippers around her. He supposed that it was as a subject for study that she gave him so keen a pleasure; but there was also some proprietary interest, he decided when he began to analyse that sentiment in his inevitable fashion. It seemed to him that she sat like a young dam master. He always spoke with bitterness and contempt, yet she invariably got the impression that other and very different emotions might lie behind. To-day his bitterness was sufficiently pronounced, even while he admitted affection and pleaded that something might be remembered in the Prince's favour. She imagined that while he contemned the subject of their conversation he would have resented, though perhaps in silence, an attack from outside. This curious loyalty, once realised, moved her admiration as well as her compassion and she gave it a generous reward.

"Mr. Herbertson," she said gently, "I have never said a word against Prince Adrian. I never saw him, and I do not even know the whole story. But I do not blame him for our misfortunes. Mathias was older than he, and was himself responsible for the course he followed. Hear me, now, and believe me! I should no more think of blaming Prince Adrian than I should think of blaming you."

Mr. Herbertson looked considerably surprised. Perhaps the whole course of his own thoughts for many days had for the first time received a check.

"You are too charitable," he murmured.

"No, I am not charitable. I am only trying to be just. And now I will try to be grateful also, Mr. Herbertson, as I must be if I claim to have a heart. If the Prince had indeed been solely responsible for our misfortunes, as you have suggested, I should still refuse a word of blame against him. Your goodness would have wiped out everything, and would have raised a heavy debt on the other side."

Mr. Herbertson was moved by the warmth and

tive Methodist bench. He discovered suddenly that the girl was watching him gravely, and he was on the alert at once to the danger of betraying his thoughts.

This danger had increased recently, for these last few days had revealed another side of her nature. It was the side which looked back towards childhood. With inexpressible delight he had found hidden in her a kindred spirit, one who could enjoy the children as he enjoyed them, and even become one of themselves as he could not do. Finding common ground in this way, their fellowship might have deepened but for his unfaltering vigilance. He could not forget who and what she was, he must not forget who and what he was. Thus his friendliness never lost an undefined but unmistakable formality, for he was always on guard.

She realised this and guessed its purpose, but while she understood it she could not be expected to discover the necessity of it. Once or twice she had tried to break it down, only to withdraw, a little more puzzled but not displeased. Doubtless he had his reasons, and her confidence in him covered everything.

To-day the special circumstances led her to make another attempt. It did not succeed, but it left a deeper confidence than before.

"When do you expect to be back, Mr. Herbertson?" she asked.

"Back? Oh, Hadfield has a fortnight's holiday," he said.

"But you hope to finish your business before the fortnight?"

"Yes. But that is not in my own hands. However, I am sure that it will not take long."

There was a pause; then she said:

"You are going into danger for us. But I wish you to know that I feel sure of your success."

There was a definite confidence and deliberation in the statement. It had been well considered. He found her eyes upon him with the same assurance in them.

"My success?"

"Yes. I feel assured of your success."

It could be nothing more than presentiment:—yet it seemed to be something more. Yet all he could say was that he was glad she felt like that about it. After all, what more could any one have said? She went on with the same deliberation:

"I think I may tell you more. You are serving my mother first, and myself because you serve her: but that is not all the story. In this matter you are serving me very greatly indeed, for you are standing between me and a man whom I fear."

Mr. Herbertson was impressed. "Do you feel in this way about him?" he said. "But it is natural. He had his share, of course, in this dastardly betrayal."

"Yes," she said, "and that would be enough. But there is more than that, and it was before that. From my childhood I have had a fear of Philip Brode, a horror, a repulsion. It was something I could not conquer. My parents could not understand it, and almost blamed me for it. He was our neighbour, not near, as your neighbours are here, but still a neighbour; but I would never have seen him if it had been possible to avoid it."

me say now that your view is too generous. I wish
you to remember always that I am doing the plain
man's duty of trying to right a wrong. I must try
by all means to restore to you the happiness of
which the folly of my master, Prince Adrian, deprived you. That is my purpose."

There was a long silence. The situation had
never been clearly stated before, though there had
been some consciousness of it. The Countess was
touched, and met his look with a new sympathy.

"Oh," she said, "but you must not say that!
You are not responsible for another man. Are you
doing it because—because you once loved him? Is
it that you would clear his name as far as you can?"

There was a long silence. "It may be that,"
was the grave answer. "There is no doubt that I
once loved him. After that I despised him, and
then I tried to forget him. Yet there is one thing
I should like you to remember when these troubles
are over and you are once again in your home."

"I shall remember many things," she answered.
"But what is this one thing?"

"It is this. But for the power of Prince Adrian's
name, I should never have gained the ear of the
Chancellor. If your misfortunes are due to him,
it may also be admitted that our present hope springs
from the same source."

"It is strange," she said musingly. "But it is
true."

"Strange and true. And if we succeed I trust
that this strange truth will not be forgotten. There
is so much on the debit side."

The Countess often found herself a little perplexed when Mr. Herbertson mentioned his quon-

"So you are taking my husband away?" she said; and Mr. Herbertson, leaning against the edge of the table, admitted the charge.

"Yes, madam. And it is very good of you to let him go."

"He needs a holiday."

"So do you, no doubt."

"No. I am having one now. Every hour of the day."

Mr. Herbertson understood, and was pleased. He noticed that Mrs. Hadfield still wore the nameless garment which had attracted his attention on the Second of May, and that it suited her equally well with the sleeves turned back to the elbows. Floury hands were not unattractive, and it was possible to display a considerable amount of grace in the manipulation of a rolling-pin. There might be the germ of an essay in this discovery. He would make a note of it when he returned to his study. Then he raised his eyes from the floury hands to meet a smile vivid in its nature and tonic in its effect. But was "vivid" the best word for the nature of that smile? He must consider this again. Meanwhile, under the tonic influence of that same smile, he proceeded to his business.

"Is the Countess ready to see me?"

"She is waiting, Mr. Herbertson. Just go in."

Mr. Herbertson went.

Mrs. Hadfield heard him go in. She proceeded with her cake-making, but her mind was with Mr. Herbertson. The problem had become much more interesting of late: and now, quite suddenly, it assumed a new aspect. How old was Mr. Herbertson? He sometimes looked forty-five or even less,

"Yes. I have called it The Garden of Security."

The man looked straight before him. It had been in turn a Garden of Illusion and a Garden of Fear. Here was a new name indeed!

"It is so well guarded," she went on. "Here is a wall of houses—your Arran Terrace—a battlement manned by the best of friends. And farther away, do you not see, there are buildings all round. So I never walk here without that feeling of Security."

She did not read in his smile any secret thought of broken reeds. And she went on:

"But are you going to stay in this garden always? It does not seem large enough."

"It gives me more work than I can do," he answered ruefully. "Look at that greenhouse."

She did not look. She was intent upon her very delicate purpose.

"I hope you will forgive me if I say too much. You have been so kind that I may perhaps be made presumptuous. But I—we—would like to see you in a larger place. Must you stay here?"

She saw his surprise, and went on impetuously. Yet so much was left unsaid. How could she explain that from the very first she had sensed some essential inconsistency between the man and his chosen sphere. Her mother had realised it too, but no one else had done so.

"Mother has spoken of it. I do hope you will forgive us both if we have done wrong. But when all this is over, and we go back— She has influence in certain circles, and already you know the country and the language—yes, and some of the leaders.

And she thought that if she could serve you in that way, and you were willing to go. . . ."

She paused. His face had hardened and darkened. She could go no further until he had spoken. He spoke with restraint, almost coldly.

"You do not know. It is quite out of the question."

"Of course I do not know," she said. "But is it that trouble of so many years ago?" And then, as he nodded: "But surely, after so long, that will be forgiven and forgotten?"

His answer was almost stern. "Was your father forgiven?"

"But he had made an enemy, and you have a powerful friend."

He had rallied from the shock, and his face had lost its shadow. Just to all, he saw that justice was not sufficient acknowledgment for the spirit which had inspired the suggestion. He spoke in his warmest tone, his hand upon her sleeve.

"My dear girl, it is quite impossible. While I can appeal to a powerful friend on your behalf, and in the name of justice, I could not appeal on my own. Besides, I haven't the slightest wish to live in Styria or to leave my garden."

That was sufficiently definite, at least, and she felt it to be final: but its harshness was mitigated by the kindness of the tone, the mode of address, used for the first time. Though she flushed she was not hurt, and her silence was not the silence of displeasure. Then Margaret Joan destroyed their privacy by coming to hide herself behind their bench, Hadfield being in search of her. But she came at the right time.

Chapter XV

The Garden Is Blotted Out, and There Are No Stars

MARJORIE HADFIELD was an extremely happy young matron. Life had been sufficiently interesting before, but now her cup seemed to overflow. The home of which she was proud with a young housewife's pride had received guests of honour whose care was her delight and whose presence was an unfailing fount of satisfaction. Moreover, Mr. Herbertson had insisted that she must have a maid, for the time at least, and a willing little girl had been added to the household to be a crown of joy. In those days Mrs. Hadfield's life was a happy dream marvellously full of business.

This was the lady who greeted Mr. Herbertson next morning, when he went in to see the Countess. Entering, by arrangement, from the garden, he was led into the kitchen, where she was making cake. As a cake-maker she made an exceedingly attractive picture, and the visitor renewed his pleasure in that dark, vivid, girlish face and its piquant, challenging expression. Her vivacity was always such a delightful contrast to the boyish stolidity of her husband.

"You see, Hadfield, things on the Continent are not as they are here. Apart from the silly political duels in France, the most ordinary cause of a duel is, of course, a dispute about a woman. One aspect of my interference in the Brode-Hamar affair amounts to this—that I have placed myself between this fiery young man and the lady he wishes to secure. Consequently, by the custom in Styria, he is entitled to challenge me."

"But you have appealed," said Hadfield.

"Quite so. But my appeal to the Chancellor concerns the restoration of the ladies to their home. My affair with young Philip is a thing apart, though not altogether apart. Since I have intervened in his somewhat peculiar courtship he is entitled to 'call me out,' and if I can give him what is called 'satisfaction' in this way, the whole business will be neatly rounded off. I shall have complied with a national custom of which I cannot profess ignorance, and he will be able to hold up his head because he has punished my interference in the only way a fire-eating Styrian officer can recognise. Is it clear now?"

It was not quite clear. "Punished?" said Hadfield. "Then it's risky?"

"Risky? My dear fellow, have you ever heard of a modern duel that ended fatally?"

Hadfield could not remember one.

"Oh," he said. "Then it's to be a mere matter of form?"

"It's to be a mere matter of form. Honour will be satisfied as long as two shots are fired, wherever the bullets go, and whether there are any bullets or not. Philip will save his face, and the great Styrian Army will have vindicated its honour. . . . And forgiveness even if he dared to hope for it at that price. After all, those stern old teachers were right: this hoary doctrine was based on a truth which the soul had learned by the lessons of ages, and events must always prove it true.

He worked it out with an awakened perception. Conscious of the flagrant wrong suffered by these women, he had gone to their rescue. He had given much, at risk to himself—he had given friendship, comfort, shelter, gifts sufficiently precious at all times in this world of need. Then he had paused, saying: "It is enough—I can do no more." But Destiny had refused to pause there, the Mills had continued their work. By a sequence of pitiless circumstances he had been led from one position to another till the Law had blazed across the sky: "Without the shedding of blood there is no remission." And now the pistol waited across the narrow sea.

It was not a comforting review, but it did not trouble him so much to-day as it might have done yesterday. There was still balm in this crowning Sabbath. Then he turned to the further note, and shook his head. *Ever so kinder.*

"No," he said. "I think Margaret Joan was wrong. The old Law stands."

For a little while he sat, staring at the page of the book but not observing it; but he saw the danger of this mood, and rose, and closed the book and put it away. Then he went to latch the French door that led to the garden.

As he closed it he looked out, but his garden was no longer visible. Darkness had slowly fallen, and blotted it out. And there were no stars.

Chapter XVI

Count Brode Tries to Comprehend the Incomprehensible

EACH act of Mr. Herbertson's drama had opened in an atmosphere of peace, however passionate the forces that awaited their call to the stage. The Fourth and last Act followed the same rule. The Garden of Security was no longer in the scene, but it had its counterpart in the natural beauty and unsuspicious quiet of that little seaside village in Normandy which Brode had chosen for the consummation of his ingenious plan.

Saint Claud, having none but the simple attractions of Nature to recommend it, was unknown to the great host of holiday-makers. Shop-keepers and modest folk from neighbouring inland towns formed the bulk of its visitors, with a small number of discriminating persons of a better class who had either discovered the place first by accident or had been recommended to it by friends. Those who came once came often, for however few its attractions, they were certainly cheap and permanent. The place was excessively clean, the bathing was good, the sands were extensive and the people were not yet perfect in the art of living upon strangers.

The Hôtel Seine was delightfully in accord with its surroundings. It was an old, whitewashed build-

"Then we'll consider it settled. That's really A.1. It will be a delight to have your company. We'll take up our quarters at a little seaside place from which we can make excursions frequently, and by the time my little affair is over, you'll have seen quite a lot of France. But come down the garden, and I'll tell you all about it."

They walked down, the wall between them, Mr. Herbertson looking so pleased that no one could have guessed his revolt against this necessary legion of lies. "But that's another thing that will be over soon," he thought. "One of the compensations of the end." And a moment later, seated once more on the Primitive Methodist bench, he shared his useful cigarettes and revealed his plans.

"I brought you down here," he explained, "because I did not wish to be overheard. A certain part of this business must be classed as 'confidential' for the present. It would be alarming because it would be misunderstood. The fact is, old fellow, that the company of a friend is very necessary, because this is not altogether a picnic. I am booked to fight a duel."

Hadfield's incredulity was sufficiently complete. "What! A duel? You?"

"Just that. Pistols for two and coffee for four, you know. And as there must be four to drink the coffee, I must have a second."

It was difficult to take him seriously, but Hadfield knew his neighbour sufficiently well to see that there might be a fact behind that frivolous manner. He reached it by a very simple bit of reasoning.

"By Jove!" he said. "That young Brode!"

"Why, you have it," cried Mr. Herbertson.

by buttressed towers: and each corner of the building also had its tower, duly battlemented. Originally these had been of a species unfamiliar to Western eyes, but on consideration the artist had replaced his first designs by structures of Norman type. There was a suggestion of a park in the foreground, and a broad stream aggressively blue.

"Yes," mused Mr. Herbertson, critically. "I think it should do. That river is so blue that it might suggest the Blue Danube. But those Norman towers—there is no such architecture on the Blue Danube!"

Another thought came: "A strong place, with strength and power all about it. A man bred in such a hold as this might be expected to breathe into his being something of that power and restraint. . . . Perhaps the fault was that he left it too soon—at fifteen or so, I believe. Then the fever and folly and fret of the Court, heady and maddening. No, Adrian, I am sure it would have been better had you stayed at home for at least a little longer. But there was no one to see to it."

The drawing was to be enclosed in a dainty leather-bound case, with Margaret's initials on the side, and a letter which Mr. Herbertson had written was to face the drawing. He now spent an absorbed hour in transcribing this letter, for it must have an initial in red, and a tailpiece ornament drawn with absurd care. That was in the original plan, but now he added extra care, the fruit of self-reproach. Having completed this task he laid the unusual gift away in his desk just as Mrs. Jenner called him. "And now," he said to himself, "you may feel a little better, having atoned by much

It was a rather awkward moment, and at first even the Count seemed at a loss. Then he spoke to his son:

"Mr. Herbertson, Philip. Here is Mr. Herbertson. Our friend has arrived."

Philip gave a nod of recognition. The Count smiled at Hadfield.

"My friend Mr. Hadfield," said Herbertson briefly. "Hadfield, you must know Herr Pasberg, of Cologne."

The Count bowed, and gave the stranger a cordial greeting. He succeeded in conveying the impression that he was sincerely glad to meet an old acquaintance and the friend of that old acquaintance; and before he had ended his little speech he had examined and classified Hadfield with confidence and precision. Then he joined his son. Hadfield sat down with Mr. Herbertson, and the waiter, having arranged the lamp to his satisfaction, went out once more. A few minutes later other guests came in and the tables had been served.

It was a curious affair at best; to Hadfield it was amazing. He had supposed that the meeting of the two parties would be a somewhat dramatic affair, and had wondered much what his own attitude should be. Instead, there was nothing more than an ordinary meeting of acquaintances, followed by the very ordinary function of the evening meal at tables separated but a few feet from each other in a pleasant window alcove overlooking garden and sea, and with an alert waiter hovering within easy call. He felt inclined to rub his eyes.

There were further marvels. The Count began to speak, and kept up a light and occasional conversation which was not the less interesting because it was light and occasional; for this evil and vengeful old man—as Hadfield had learned to regard him —was a master of the art of speech. Even against his own will the young fellow was drawn into the talk, and now and again Philip joined, though conversation was evidently not in his equipment. So the moments passed easily, and, what was more surprising still, pleasantly.

"Herbertson told me," thought Hadfield, "that this affair was to be only a mere matter of form, and it is. I expected thunder, but I had forgotten. It isn't done in these days and among these people!"

So he adjusted his impressions, feeling some surprise that Herbertson was not a little more free also. Perhaps, however, it would hardly be the thing for the two principals to treat the business so lightly as that. Form was form, after all, even if it were nothing more.

His conclusions were confirmed when the Count turned his chair, making a distant third at their table. The meal was now over, and the few guests had gone.

"Perhaps," he said, "it would be well to speak of our little affair now, since we are together. Pardon me, Mr. Herbertson, but would you leave it to Mr. Hadfield and myself, or shall we speak of it in company?"

Mr. Herbertson answered at once: "I think we may speak of it together, and this time is as good as any."

"Decidedly," agreed the Count, and he produced a case of cigarettes, and offered it to the newcomers. Herbertson smiled and refused, and Hadfield, after a moment's hesitation, accepted. Then, leaning forward in his chair, the Count spoke in a lower tone; but the difference in tone made no difference in the suavity of his manner.

"This may be supposed to be a business conference," he said. "You are English customers of ours, meeting us here by arrangement. It was necessary, or at least advisable, to have some such pretext."

"It is a very good one," said Mr. Herbertson; and the Count proceeded with his story.

"First," he said, "I have to explain our choice of this place. It seemed to us, gentlemen, that it would be best not to have any public attention for our affair, such as would be given to a duel under ordinary conditions. The thing could be done quietly, and if it should happen that any injury befell, it seemed best to let it have the appearance of accident. You see the benefits of this?"

Mr. Herbertson nodded. The Count went on:

"While considering this point, I thought of Saint Claud. It happens that an acquaintance of mine— it matters not who—came to this place some four years ago with a sick daughter who needed rest and quiet. It was very slow for this person, but he chanced to be an expert with the pistols; and in those days of idleness he was in the habit of going out to the rocks beyond the hotel and making practice there. This was an interesting pastime for empty hours, and several other visitors were drawn to take part in it. In brief it became quite popular, and the tradition remained after my friend had left. I have ascertained from our host that even last year some of his guests amused them-

selves in this way; and after hearing this we remarked that it would suit us also.   We have both
had Army training, of course.   Accordingly I sent
to Tréport for pistols and a couple of air-guns,
which arrived this morning; and it would be the
most natural thing in the world if you chanced to
join us on one or two occasions at pistol practice."

The Count paused, smiling.   "And this little business," he went on, "can easily be arranged for an
evening later—some time when we shall have no
spectators.   It can all be done in just three minutes
—and honour will be satisfied."

There was silence for a moment; each, apparently, waited for another to speak.

"That is our little plan, gentlemen," said the
Count.   "What do you say of it?"

His glance rested on the face of Mr. Herbertson
as he waited for an answer.   Philip, too, was looking at his opponent, puzzled that his father should
consider this nobody worth the inconvenience of a
visit to such a place as Saint Claud.   He only wondered, however—it would have been too fatiguing
to think—and his father would not explain until
he chose to do so.

Mr. Herbertson made an effort to rise to the
occasion, but Hadfield was conscious of the constraint of his friend's manner.   It almost nullified
the heroic efforts of the Count to make matters
smooth.

"It will do as well as any other," he said.   "It
is very ingenious.   We concur entirely.   Is there
anything more?"

The Count took the question as a hint.   He rose
placidly.

"Nothing more," he answered. "The rest can be settled another time. It gives us pleasure that you approve."

All rose at this point, and the two parties separated. "We will take a walk on the sands, Hadfield," said Mr. Herbertson; and they passed out to the hall. Hadfield looked back as they reached the door, embarrassed a little by his companion's curtness; and as he looked back he found that Count Brode was watching their departure. The suave old gentleman gave a friendly nod, and it would have been very far from Hadfield's mind just then to suggest that there was anything cruel or hawk-like in his face or expression. It was difficult to believe that this man could have brought that cruel doom upon the Hamars.

They took the path leading down from the cliff. It was now late, and the sea and sands lay in a clear moonlight which seemed to emphasise the stillness. Two fishermen, walking from the sea towards the village, conversed in deep tones as they walked. Their shadows kept pace with them, gigantic and grotesque, at their feet.

Hadfield had been ruminating. "It's rather fortunate that this is only a matter of form," he said presently. "That Philip looks a Tartar."

"He *is* a Tartar," said Herbertson. "You'll find the Tartar type all through Lusia, sometimes amazingly emphasised. Oh, they had a good run there, did the Tartars, and as they borrowed the Lusian women as a matter of course, they left their mark in the country for ever. Philip is a reversion to type. All the Tartar strain in a long line seems to have chosen him to make a final flourish. He isn't a bit like his father. The mind is altogether lacking."

Hadfield was amused. He knew nothing of racial phenomena, and had used the phrase colloquially.

"But no, I'm wrong," added Herbertson, after a pause for acid thought. "Philip is his father, after all—minus the veneer and the mind. He is all the Tartar in his father, and that's a good bit; but he has collected all the rest of the Tartar heritage as well. I fancy the Count must study his son with mixed feelings!"

"They seem to get on well together."

"They do, when they are together. Brode handles his Tartar as skilfully as he handles everyone else. I think he is really fond of him in a way. It's his own Tartar, you see. But it isn't likely that his fondness will ever have any response. In the Tartar even the cub is not playful or affectionate."

Herbertson had evidently been taking notes. Hadfield, out of his depth, found his footing in a confession.

"I'm jolly glad he didn't come to Arran Terrace. I shouldn't care to tackle him. Your way is the best."

"I hope so!" said Herbertson.

"What do you think of the plan?"

"It is a very clever plan," said the other, "yet very simple. Yes, it is a very good plan."

And he saw that it was. Four gentlemen staying at the "Seine" amuse themselves with pistol practice, a frequent pastime at Saint Claud. One evening an accident occurs, and there is some little commotion locally; but there is no breath of suspicion, for there is really no ground for suspicion. In the result one obscure Englishman is laid aside. Mr. Herbertson saw that his enemy had arranged to give him what might be described as a dog's death—a single shot in a corner among the rocks. The old man had had freedom to make his own plans, and they were as fine as thread but strong as steel.

The victim had made a feeble attempt to save a little of the game—to snatch one trophy from the disaster. How ineffective that move seemed now, the move that had taxed every power of which he was possessed; how inevitable and inexorable the repulse and the scorn, the hurried, crestfallen return.

The thought was too unnerving, and he tried to thrust it aside. His source of courage was the remembrance of those for whom he was acting, and the reflection that victory was possible—just possible—while the sacrifice was the only way. So he kept this before him as they crossed the sands.

Count Brode and Philip watched them from the window, the younger man with the sullen look that was habitual to him. Saint Claud bored him, for there were no women here of the kind that interested him; and Mr. Herbertson bored him, and Hadfield bored him, not to mention the Hôtel Seine and its obsequious landlord. His father bored him too at times. The older man was so full of schemes and plans, so rich in intrigue, so fond of contest with other minds. The young man lived only for to-day and to-morrow, and the mind that found its favourite studies in triumphs that were ten years behind or five years before was a thing that oppressed him. Besides, he was so secretive! But the duel promised a trifling sensation, and there was one epithet to be punished in the only way possible.

At the present moment he was considering a fact which had presented itself with all the effects of a surprise. He expressed that surprise without tact.

"So he came to Saint Claud," he said suddenly. "You thought he would not."

The Count smiled wisely. "What mistakes I sometimes make," he murmured. "I am growing old, Philip! Nevertheless to come to Saint Claud is not to face the pistol."

"You did not expect him to bring a companion?"

"No. But the companion will not matter."

Philip agreed with a nod. He, too, had classified poor George. "It is to give himself a little courage," said the Count, unerring in his diagnosis. "It is amusing. I must see what I can do with Mr. Hadfield. At least he will help us to pass the time."

There was a brief silence, during which Philip exercised his thoughts. But that problem was too much for him unaided, and he yawned. Then came another question:

"Well, when shall it come to pass?"

"That is not decided. I had to wait until they came."

"But I hope you will not delay it long."

"Why?" asked the Count.

"Because this place is hell to me."

Brode did not exhibit surprise or annoyance. He had trained himself too well. But he had received a check which was a little disconcerting. Absorbed in his expectations, all of a pleasant character, he had failed to give sufficient consideration to the feelings of his necessary instrument. He quickly adjusted himself to this situation.

"It is very dull," he said. "But you need not remain here all the time. It is not even necessary that you should be here every evening. But we must not too greatly hasten the affair. If it took place immediately it would surely awaken suspicion."

Philip acquiesced somewhat unwillingly. "A few days, then," he muttered.

"Probably not more. We will arrange according to circumstances. While the time must not be too short, neither should it be too long. The people here understand that while I need a brief rest by the sea I also meet these English correspondents to discuss a little business. Perhaps a week should be a reasonable time."

"It will do," said Philip. "Though no time is reasonable for such a place as this. I go to Tréport in the morning."

"Good. And I shall stay here to meditate and to enjoy the neighbourhood of Mr. Herbertson. Having been deprived of it for so many years, and being about to deprive myself again so soon, I must make the best of the opportunity."

So said the skilful plotter, as he watched his victim move among the shadows across the sands. Yet if he had said all he might have admitted that this business was not quite as he had expected it to be. Not that he was definitely dissatisfied with things as they were; but Mr. Herbertson had come to Saint Claud. That fact introduced into the affair—although he had made every preparation for it—just that element of the incomprehensible which every skilled plotter hates and fears.

Chapter XVII

—And Refuses to Accept the Pipe of Peace

THEY were strange days, those days at Saint Claud, so restful superficially, so charged with hidden forces of violence and passion. They were days of a curious isolation, for the two men had not been able to leave any address to which letters might be sent, and at present they could not write any letters. The new world was an unfamiliar one after the quiet streets of Waldington, the peopled privacy of Arran Terrace and the crowded garden behind Number Four. The people were strange too, amiable enough in every way, but foreign in all things and therefore to a large extent creatures of another realm.

To Hadfield, however, the new world was a delightful one, for he was not aware of its realities. He had never been abroad before, and every person, place and circumstance was vivid with interest for him. Within its limits the Seine was luxurious, and its proprietor, Henri Barbier, was a character in whom he found some new facet of delight at every laboured conversation. There was a waiter, too, who had sole charge of the dining-room at this time. He was a Swiss, he said, and had spent some

233

months in London to acquire English. He had learned sufficient English to serve many purposes, and as he desired to acquire more, he paid special attention to the most definitely English of all the guests. George spent several informative half-hours with Rudolf when Mr. Herbertson was not available, and always left him with a sense of satisfaction in the miscellaneous knowledge he had garnered and the English lessons he had given in exchange.

Mr. Herbertson, of course, exerted himself to secure that Hadfield should enjoy the holiday. It seemed to him that it was taking an unfair advantage of his good-natured friend to use him as a cloak for suicidal sacrifice, and to leave him afterwards with a dead man to dispose of, so he made those first days as happy as possible. He searched out all the places of interest in the district, and appointed himself cicerone; he gave George various lessons in French, and what was equally good, he made an excellent listener when the young man chose to talk. This favourable atmosphere could scarcely be resisted, and George Hadfield probably talked more in those few days than he would do ordinarily in as many weeks. He talked of his office, of his home and family at a farm three miles out of Waldington, and most of all of his wife. And there they found an excellent meeting place, for Mr. Herbertson showed plainly that he had a profound admiration for Marjorie, mingled with some noble envy of the man who was so fortunate as to possess her. Then George told Mr. Herbertson that his esteem was reciprocated.

"She thinks no end of you," he said. "Almost the

last thing she told me was that I must take the utmost care of you. *Me*—to take care of *you!*"

"That was very good of her," said Mr. Herbertson. "Was she under the impression that I should run into danger?"

"I don't really know. But she was very particular about it. She actually said that I wasn't to let you get out of my sight. What do you think of that?"

"I think a great deal of it," said his friend.

"She couldn't have guessed anything about this duel business," said Hadfield. "I was very careful not to let a hint escape. But that's just like Madge. She seems to jump at things, without knowing how."

"Intuition," murmured Mr. Herbertson. "But I hope you will carry out her orders in a worthy manner."

Hadfield smiled. "It would be hard lines on me if I went back without you," he said. "I know that." At which Mr. Herbertson smiled also, but not quite so happily.

During the first days he had one interview with Count Brode alone—one which was inevitable, and which he had foreseen with dread and abhorrence. It took place in the evening, after dinner, when Philip had gone to Tréport. It had been a somewhat silent dinner, the Count providing most of the occasional intercourse between the two tables and Hadfield providing most of the attention. As the room began to clear, however, Count Brode turned to Herbertson.

"If your friend will excuse us," he said, "we can do our little business within the next half-hour. Is the time quite convenient for you—and this place?"

"Entirely so," said Mr. Herbertson. "Hadfield, you can run away and play. I will join you presently."

Hadfield laughed and vanished. The Count went to his room and returned with a small portfolio. He sat at the table opposite Mr. Herbertson, so that the light from the window might fall between them, and so that he might watch his victim's face. "Leave this table for a while, Rudolf," he said, when the waiter came near; and to Mr. Herbertson, as the man withdrew: "These Swiss have some knowledge of all tongues, but are perfect in none. Still, it is just as well that he should not disturb us. And I have brought these papers so that we may seem to be discussing business."

He spread the papers out upon the table, first pushing various utensils aside. By this time the few diners had gone. Mr. Herbertson, as we have seen, had looked forward to this interview with dread and abhorrence, but now he found that though the abhorrence remained the dread had disappeared. He was not afraid. Was it because he had passed through so many painful experiences since their meeting in the Petersburg? Watching the strong white hands arrange the papers, he wondered.

"Now we can get on," said the Count. "I am sorry to trouble you, Mr. Herbertson, but it is necessary. I am anxious to know what arrangements you have made on your part—in case of accident."

Mr. Herbertson looked up into his eyes. It cost him an effort to do it. The clash was instant, but he maintained his front to the end. Those brilliant black eyes, alert to every motion, steady and pitiless beneath that heavy brow and inconsistent eyebrows, failed to mark anything that might be described as faltering. His voice was firm.

"My part shall be thoroughly performed," he said. "My friend has come with me for various reasons, but one of them is that he may make things easy. He asks no questions, he knows nothing of the truth. He believes that the meeting is to be purely formal—a mere exchange of shots. But I will give him a letter, and will instruct him to open it immediately if any 'accident' should occur. It will tell him what to do and what not to do. He will not be the source of any trouble. I guarantee that."

"Good," said Count Brode. "And there is no one else in England who knows anything?"

"No one who even guesses anything. And no one must know after. That was a condition—that my secret should be kept?"

"It was," said the Count, "and we will keep every condition."

"It is very fortunate that to some extent our interests are identical," said Herbertson, calmly.

There was a pause during which the older man adjusted his conceptions of the situation. The victim was desperate, and would sting if he could.

"Yes," he said. "You put it admirably. To some extent our interests are identical. And as you keep your items of the contract, so will we keep ours."

Mr. Herbertson knew better; but he did not reply. The Count took up a paper and laid it down again. "May I enquire if you have followed affairs in Styria of late years?" he asked.

"Not closely," answered the victim. "I wished to forget. But I have noticed the name of Brode in the press."

"It gratifies me that you have condescended to notice," murmured the Count. "And you have observed the elevation of one who was the friend of your friend?"

"Baron Ronnefeldt," answered Herbertson, "has gained the esteem of the whole world—and has deserved it."

Count Brode inclined his head mockingly. That answer had been quite in harmony with his conclusions. He decided to push his provocation a little more strongly, and leaned forward over the papers. Herbertson was sitting as at first, nonchalantly, one elbow upon the table. The fish upon the hook was more at ease than the older man had expected; but it must be a pose. It could be nothing more.

"I am wondering if you would answer a somewhat intimate question, Mr. Herbertson?" he said smoothly.

"Ask it."

"Thank you, Mr. Herbertson. Then I must confess to a little curiosity on one incident of the past. How did you come to the resolve to put our mutual friend out of the way?"

Probably the Count did not expect an answer to the question. "That is not within the contract, I think," said Mr. Herbertson.

"I accept the rebuke," said the Count, entirely unperturbed. "But after all it is not difficult to imagine what your reasons were. Our mutual friend must have been a considerable problem to his companion and to himself; and a person who is a problem, a trial, and a responsibility may soon find his very existence in danger."

Mr. Herbertson did not reply, nor did he show signs of any special discomfort. For a few moments the Count studied that pale but well-controlled countenance; then he proceeded in the same tone of mockery veiled by suavity.

"And may I ask how you have lived since that time? Have you been happy? Was there no spectre to trouble you?"

"There have been spectres. But I had a garden."

"A garden?"

"Yes. A garden."

The two men were eye to eye again. Mr. Herbertson seemed to be even a little amused. It was a mood which his enemy could not understand.

"It is a very small garden," he said. "Not half an acre in all. Less than a pocket-handkerchief. But I do most of the work in this garden myself. And I confidently recommend the work of a garden, Count, to any man troubled by unhealthy humours, memories, or regrets. If he cannot avoid them it will help him to bear them; moreover, it will keep him so busy that he will be unable to work much evil in the world outside."

"This is very interesting, Mr. Herbertson. Let me hear a little more of your philosophy."

"There is no more. The application of the philosophy I leave to you."

The Count smiled grimly. "Yes," he said. "You think it would be well for me to be in a garden—

or under it. Unfortunately for you, Mr. Herbertson, I am here, and you have had to come out of your garden to meet me here."

He enjoyed the retort at the time. Later he was dissatisfied with it. Mr. Herbertson watched his enjoyment, however, without discomposure. Having discovered that he was not afraid he found also that other emotions were seeking a place in his consciousness. The reference to the garden was responsible to some degree, but even before that he had experienced something far removed from dread and abhorrence. Could it be pity? Impossible, surely! Was it contempt? That was more likely. But with the thought of the garden the harshness of contempt passed too, and pity was left to reign alone and undisguised. This old man had power and place, with capacity far beyond the ordinary, but he was now bending all his energies to making revenge a fine art and crowning it with murder. Mr. Herbertson looked into his eyes again, and there was something in his own that the enemy could not name.

"It was not a misfortune that I came out of my garden," he said very deliberately. "At least, I believe that it was not. The story is not yet ended. But since we are speaking together, Count Brode, in this frank way, I will take the liberty, or the opportunity, of making a request—or perhaps an appeal."

"An appeal, Mr. Herbertson? Come, this is even more interesting than your philosophy. Proceed."

"I beg of you, then, to abandon the project which has brought us here."

Now Count Brode thought he recognised that unnamed look. He misnamed it fear. He answered the appeal with a semblance of seriousness. Mr. Herbertson went on:

"I offer no reasons. But if it will make it more possible for your son to abandon the duel, I will withdraw any remarks which may have wounded him during our interview at the Petersburg."

That was all. Mr. Herbertson had known the folly of such a step, its crass absurdity. As usefully might the fascinated bird appeal to the basilisk. Having spoken, he turned his eyes away from that mocking face and looked out to the sea. There was a long silence, a silence deliberately prolonged by the man who had to give the answer. At last he gave it:

"May I ask, Mr. Herbertson, if you got that suggestion out of your garden? If you did, that pocket-handkerchief is capable of strange crops."

Mr. Herbertson did not reply. The Count opened a cigarette-case and extended it over the table.

"My reply is to ask you to take a cigarette. But you must not mistake it for the pipe of peace."

Mr. Herbertson did not take a cigarette. "I have said all that I have to say," he replied. "Is there any purpose in talking further?"

"None at all," said the Count, lighting a cigarette for himself and sweeping his papers into their folder. "I am indebted to you, above all for your appeal. That alone will make the interview distinctive and memorable. And I bid you good evening, Mr. Herbertson."

He left the room with that deferential air which

emphasised his mockery, and Mr. Herbertson was left alone in profound relief that this ordeal at last was over.

The absurdity of his appeal troubled him a little and amused him a little, but it satisfied some sense which he was in the habit of satisfying. That was the first of two notable items in the interview, and it left him with mingled discomfort and satisfaction. The other item was the discovery that he had not suffered any fear such as he had known at the Petersburg. This was a cause for astonishment indeed, and something akin to joy. He had looked Death in the face and had felt little more than a quickening of the pulses. Could this be true? Seeking reasons for his lack of fear, he reflected that he was no longer a young man. "At twenty," he said to himself, "death is the greatest of the whole catalogue of possible evils. At five and forty, life, already more than half gone, has relaxed its hold, while Death, having become more and more a familiar idea, has lost half its terrors."

There were periods, however, when his weaker self prevailed, and then those quiet days became charged with tempest. That was when this calculated sacrifice, this evilly-planned murder, filled him with unutterable bitterness, resentment and revolt. And the thing he had to lean upon was a chance—a feeble chance which would probably come to nothing—that an old man, seven hundred miles away, would consider his ridiculous standard of honour satisfied!

Once, while in this mood, he walked to the nearest railway station, some distance from the village, drawn to look upon the means which could, if he so wished, take him out of this astounding situation. For a while he lingered about there idly, but when a train was signalled he saw himself in danger, and returned to Saint Claud in a rage of shame and self-accusation. Before he reached the village he met Philip Brode, who was taking a stroll in the same direction, and the sight of that sullen face completed the reaction.

Mr. Herbertson did not go to the station again. He saw that he must guard against such moods as this. His great fear was that his weakness might overwhelm him and bring his aspirations to disaster.

On the Tuesday evening the Brodes put their plan into operation, and told Hadfield that they would take a little pistol practice among the rocks about a quarter of a mile beyond the hotel.

"Shall we go?" asked Hadfield of his companion.

"There is no need for both of us to go," answered Mr. Herbertson. "Go yourself. That will be quite as well."

Hadfield went, not at all reluctantly. On his return at dusk he gave his report.

"It was not bad sport," he said. "Several people heard the firing and came to look on. I tried a little myself, but of course I couldn't make any kind of show, even with an air-gun. The Count was first-rate; he made no end of hits, without any trouble at all. But as for his son—well, I must say he doesn't seem much of a hand at it. If he did hit anything in a duel it would be more of an accident than anything else!"

Mr. Herbertson smiled at his friend's simplicity. He did not tell him that Philip was by repute the best shot in the Styrian army.

"By the way," continued Hadfield, "I never asked you, are you anything of a shot yourself?"

"I haven't fired a pistol twice in my life."

"No? By Jove! Hadn't you better try, then?"

"Why should I?" asked Mr. Herbertson. "As you know, the whole thing is only a matter of form. Besides, in case of accident it would certainly be more useful if one of the party were a novice. People would be able to say, 'It serves him right for playing with firearms.'"

Hadfield laughed as he saw the force of this argument, which he did not succeed in shaking. He was relieved, however, to find that the Count received his explanations with perfect good humour when they chanced to meet an hour later.

"After all," said the old man, with irony which Hadfield did not see—"after all, Mr. Herbertson is perhaps right. It will be quite enough if he only comes here once."

"Of course it will," agreed Hadfield. "Nothing more is required."

"No," said the Count dryly, "nothing more."

This understanding might have seemed satisfactory to all parties, but the person who had expressed the greatest satisfaction was the one who liked it least. It gave Count Brode food for thought. It was obvious that Mr. Herbertson was in a condition of terror, otherwise he would not have refused a part in the game. That, of course, was just as it should be; but the Count, who was watching his victim closely, could not feel that all the circumstances justified him in adopting the obvious and satisfactory conclusion. Certainly Mr. Herbertson gave indications of concern at times—signs which the Count could read easily enough; but it seemed to him that at other times he was not at all afraid. That extraordinary interview, too, had been only superficially satisfactory, and the old man recalled it with an uneasiness which was none the less real because he could not define it. "He means to fly," he muttered, "and since he will not face the pistol he does not need to fear. . . ." But though this explanation was plausible he did not feel entirely satisfied.

His uncertainty bred irritation, and his irritation cruelty; and in the slow march of those few days his venom mounted higher than ever. On the Thursday afternoon he took a solitary walk, during the course of which he examined the situation in every aspect and found it satisfactory. That one element of uncertainty was capable of explanation; and the only thing he regarded as absolutely impossible was the thing that had actually occurred. He did not miss the suggestion that Mr. Herbertson might have lodged an appeal at Graaden; but having examined it, he thrust it aside with contempt.

"No," he said decisively, "that is out of the question."

Having thus cleared the way he resolved to bring the business to a speedy end. He had intended to prolong it, and had promised himself much pleasure from that source; but his own irritation endorsed his son's impatience, and he determined to pluck his fruit at once. So he returned to the hotel with a more settled mind, and on that evening announced his decision. Saturday was to be the day: and the English visitors to the Seine would give out that they would probably leave on the Monday.

Hadfield, of course, agreed. "We will arrange," said the Count, "to be out here on Saturday a little earlier, just before people go to the beach for the evening. When we come we shall have forgotten some trifle, and will send our attendant back to the hotel for it. During the half-hour of his absence, everything can be done. Will you speak to Mr. Herbertson?"

"Of course," said Hadfield. "I am sure, Count, that he will be quite agreeable to anything you suggest."

How confident this young man was! What would he say if he found his principal wanting when the time came?

"Very good, Mr. Hadfield," he said. "I suggest, further, that we must not all come together, as that would indicate prearrangement. Let it be that you and Mr. Herbertson come first. We will follow almost immediately with the cases."

"That is excellent," was Hadfield's reply. "I am sure there will be no difficulty."

For a little while no more was said. Presently they brought their practice to an end, somewhat to the disappointment of the idlers who were watching it, and prepared to return to the hotel. It was then that the Count placed himself at Hadfield's side. The old man had still a little more to do to perfect his vengeance, and here was his opportunity. He was not satisfied that his enemy should be slain. He must go to death without a single friend.

Chapter XVIII

Mr. Herbertson Dreams of an Old Sword

"MY dear Mr. Hadfield," he began, in a way that was most flattering, "it has been upon my mind to give you my confidence. Will you forgive me if I dare to speak plainly?"

Hadfield could only look surprised. The Count, however, did not require permission to go on.

"I am desirous," he said gently, "that both my son and myself should stand well with you—that you should not regard us with unjust ideas. I imagine that Mr. Herbertson has told you one version of this business already.—No, no—I am not asking you what he said. I am only anxious that you should have a glimpse of the other side. The duel, of course, is not to be considered—it is a mere matter of appearances. But I may not have an opportunity of speaking with you again, and I do not wish that you should return to England with only one story in your mind. May I hope that you understand me?"

"Certainly, Count," stammered Hadfield, who was far from comprehending.

"Excellent! I felt that I had not misread you! And now, my friend, I have no doubt that in your heart you think me cruel for forcing your companion to submit to this ordeal—a man to whom such an ordeal is not easy, even when it is only a form. Let

247

me explain, then, that we are justified. We have good reason. More, if you knew all you would be amazed that we do no more than this—that we do not seek to inflict a more adequate punishment."

"Punishment?" echoed Hadfield, bewildered.

The Count had suddenly become very grave. "Punishment," he repeated with solemn emphasis; and there he paused.

They walked on for a few paces before he proceeded; and in the meantime the meaning of the word punishment, or rather a suggestion of its meaning, had grown in Hadfield's mind, and he was ready for the application.

"Mr. Hadfield," said the old man, "it is not my wish to betray your friend's secrets. I refuse to do so. Since he has decided to carry out my conditions it would not be honourable. And yet I also must be defended from misunderstanding.—But before I go further I must have your promise that what passes now is strictly in confidence. It must not go to Mr. Herbertson."

"Certainly not," murmured Hadfield, with the readiness of credulity and good-will. "It is entirely between ourselves, Count."

"Just so. Between ourselves. Then, Mr. Hadfield, I ask you this. If you doubt our right to punish, or the mildness of the punishment, make enquiries for yourself. Find out from your friend, now or later—find out in some other way if he will not tell you—find out *how Prince Adrian died!*"

That was all. The last words were spoken in a low tone just as they turned the corner of the cliff to reach the path to the hotel. "Ah! here we are," said the Count, almost in the same breath.

"Thank you, Mr. Hadfield. The arrangements are now in your hands. I am sure you will do everything well."

He turned with a parting smile to wait for his son. Hadfield went slowly up the path into the hotel, and straight to his room.

A thundercloud had suddenly covered his sky. He wanted to be alone to think, and he remained alone for almost an hour. Then he came down and went out to find Mr. Herbertson.

Down at the edge of the water three little French boys were splashing about with shrill cries of enjoyment, and the setting sun was red in the west. Mr. Herbertson had paused in his march across the sands to watch them, interested more in their play than in his own perilous affairs. He came up to meet his companion.

"Well?" he said, in an unconcerned way. "Any news?"

"Yes," said Hadfield. "It is to be to-morrow evening."

He described the arrangement which had been made, and Mr. Herbertson listened with close attention. Before the end he became conscious of the fact that something had taken place, and then it did not take him long to see that he was now alone. The Count had come between him and his last friend.

At first he felt angry and mortified, and more. He felt a sharp pang of something like despair, and the pang brought with it an echo of one of the saddest records in human history: *And they all forsook Him and fled.* But, strangely enough, that memory had a tonic effect, and he took control of the situation. Perhaps this added pain would help to fill the measure of his atonement. All that was necessary was to keep Hadfield with him to the end.

"Hadfield," he said suddenly, "I see that Count Brode has been speaking to you."

"He has," said Hadfield bluntly, but with a swift hope. Was the man going to defend himself?

"Well," said Mr. Herbertson, "I am not concerned with what he told you or what he hinted. He could not have told you anything worse than the truth. But I ask you to do one thing—to suspend judgment for a while, and stay and see the business out. I do not wish to be left alone at this point."

Hadfield's generous impulses responded at once to the appeal, in spite of the poison in his mind. That fearful suggestion—well, in Mr. Herbertson's presence it did not seem quite so fearful as it had seemed before, despite the confirmation it found in his own memory.

"Consent," said Herbertson, "to stay until the thing is over. You will then be free to do as you please. It is only another twenty-four hours—or less."

"You may depend upon me," said Hadfield, with constraint but with sincerity.

"Thank you. I knew that I could. And now we'll go in to dinner."

They went in to dinner, where the two parties met just as they had met several times in the interval; and the Count, seated with his face towards Mr. Herbertson, chatted in his pleasantest humour. The old gentleman could not fail to notice Hadfield's constraint, and there is no doubt that he enjoyed his meal exceedingly.

In due course Mr. Herbertson went upstairs to bed. It was not to be expected that a man in his extremity, his heart the field of a mortal struggle, should enjoy a night of untroubled sleep. He knew, indeed, that he could not expect it, but his chief dread was that he might not sleep at all. In that case the morning might find him hopelessly shaken, utterly unfit to meet the demands of his last day. Thus it was with a great gratitude that he found the oblivion of sleep stealing upon his senses as surely as the tide stole in upon the sands without; and he surrendered to it with the thought that this, too, might be a gift from his garden. There healthy sleep had been one of the blessings of his ordered life, only lost when some incident had stirred the hornet-nest of old memories and dreads. Yes, this was a gift from his garden, one of the most precious of many. . . .

Then he heard a cry, a cry full of the urgency of terror. It thrilled him to a sudden tensity of wakefulness, an awful anxiety. The cry came, or seemed to come, from the top of the cliff beyond Saint Claud, the cliff that had no path to its summit. He was on the beach below when he heard it, and he was dressed in those old gardening clothes which Margaret Joan had begged of him. And it was almost dark.

The cry came only once, but he did not wait for a second call. It had scarcely ceased to echo in his ears before he was making his way up the face of the cliff, his heart a tumult of wild excitement.

No living man could have scaled such a cliff, but we do such things in dreams. The shrubs that whipped his face made him a ladder, the stones that went spinning down behind him had first given him a foothold on the mad upward way. Hands and face and feet were torn and bleeding, and the sweat rolled down into his eyes and within his ragged garments. But when he was at the last extremity, his heart bursting, his breath gone, his torn hands void of all feeling, he came to the summit, and knelt there to listen and to breathe. And there in the darkness a hand touched him, some familiar fragrance came about him, and a hushed voice spoke:

"I knew you would come!"

At that voice and touch how quickly he recovered! "I am here," he panted. "Why did you call?"

"It is the Fear," she replied. "It comes nearer every moment."

There was a sob in the voice. He sought and found the hand which had touched him, and held it. It was cold and trembling when he took it, but the trembling ceased at once. He tried to warm the hand within his own. But in a moment she spoke again, wonderingly:

"Your hands are wet. They are bleeding!"

"It is the Law," he replied. "Without the shedding of blood there is no remission."

Then a hush fell upon them both. With clasped hands they waited in the dark, and in the dark the Fear approached. There was no voice, no sound but a low stirring as of a breeze among leaves, and a breath of cold. The Fear was the greater in that they could not see it. Then, remembering that her fear must be greater than his, he drew her nearer, until he felt her hair upon his face, the hair that was sometimes the aureole of a goddess. He released her hand to place his left arm about her, and with a sigh she nestled into its shelter. He felt her heart beating stormily, but as soon as his hand touched that place the storm seemed to be stilled; but something passed through, by the contact, to his own heart, and he was suddenly strong. He said:

"If there were only a place where you might shelter! It is so dark. I cannot see."

"There is a building," she whispered. "Look."

He seemed to look; and slowly out of the darkness loomed the greenhouse of his home garden. Now, however, it was finished, and the windows from the old chapel were fitted into place. But when he saw what it was he smiled.

"There is no protection in that," he said. "It is of glass, and if a stone were thrown—"

"Oh, but it does not matter," she whispered. "I am not afraid now. Your arm is enough."

In his heart the man groaned, for he knew the weakness of that reed. "If only I had a weapon!" he murmured; and she answered the murmur:

"I knew you would come," she said, "but I did not know that you would come that way. In my dreams you carried a sword, and the sword was Judgment and Deliverance."

"What wonders are you speaking?" he replied. "That was a dream indeed. That old sword hung in the hall of the Castle of Zell, where my poor Prince spent his boyhood. It was said to be the sword of the Hospodar, old Simon Zenandra, who drove the Turks out of Zell and founded the castle. It had Judgment engraved on the one side of the blade and Deliverance on the other, and it was so great that very few men could wield it."

"But you can wield it," she said. "For now I see that you hold it in your hand. It must be meant for you."

Then he perceived that he held a sword, an old sword, cross-hilted and very weighty. The mighty blade glimmered in the darkness faintly, and he could just distinguish the outline of the ancient lettering that spelt Deliverance. In his wonder he could not protest again, but gripped the enormous hilt, and with his other arm drew her nearer. And as the Fear advanced upon them stealthily, he breathed in the fragrance of her hair, and rejoiced in the warmth of her cheek against his, and felt her heart beat in unison with his own. And he knew that he would never be afraid again—never!

Now the Fear was all about them, yet it did not fall upon them, and he wondered why. And as though soul spoke to soul in the silence, so well they knew each other, she answered his wondering:

"It is the Shadow," she whispered. "It is over us, and it seems to guard us. And it is a very Big Shadow."

Then she put her arm about his neck; and as he felt the gentle hand brush his cheek his emotion became so great that he could not contain it. He gave a sob, and shook, and the sob broke through the spell of his dream, so that he woke in his bed with a little cry, and with joy that was so keen that it was a pain. Then he sat up, trembling, and knew where he was; but the joy was there still, for still he felt the touch of her hand, and the warmth of her cheek, and the fragrance of her hair and her breath. But that was a dream, for the house was still, and the voice of the Fear was the murmur of the tide as it crept softly over the sands towards the village.

For a little time he lay, listening, and piecing together the mosaic of that dream. As he did so he found that his fear was really gone, so great was the power of some other feeling that had been strengthened and intensified by the spell of the dream. He thought it was pity, with its roots deep in remorse and regret. Nor was this all, for in the flood of that emotion a familiar thought took on a larger meaning. He was to give his life to-morrow to right a wrong, and he had thought it a great thing to give. He had even thought it too much to give. Now he saw that it was a stained and broken and worthless thing which he should be ashamed to offer. He had yet dared to bargain with it, claiming a hearing from a great-souled man like Ronnefeldt, a sublime spirit like Ferdinand of Styria! Oh, the shame of it! Ah, he knew the shame of it with that girl's breath about him, her heart beating beneath his hand. He had dared to hope to save her with such an all as he had to give!

More he saw, reading one of the great riddles of humanity in the light of his own experience. When man is really awakened he knows that he has nothing that can make adequate recompense. How can a guilty life be a just offering for a pure one, even if it is given to the uttermost? So to the soul of man comes the conception of a Sacrifice that shall be sufficient, because it is infinitely more than man and because it is pure; and upon a little hill at the world's heart rises a Cross where a sinless God shall do what man can never do for himself, a Mystery that points out for ever the heinousness of sin and the hopelessness of seeking to blot it out by human endeavour.

So he saw it in the silence of that last night, and shuddered at the hopelessness of his errand. No, nothing that he could do or give could ever be set in the balance for those women—that woman. No blood of his could win remission. Yet it was all that he had to give; and in his helplessness he spoke from his heart to that Power which he had himself declared to be inexorable justice:

"It is not worthy. I know it is not worthy. But it is all that I have to give. And if You are Ever so Kinder, perhaps You will accept this unworthy thing and let it save them."

Except for the moaning of the tide the night was very quiet, and there was no answer. That Power does not speak in the wind or tide, in clouds or stars, though it sometimes utters its truths through the lips of little children.

.   .   .   .

At an earlier hour of that evening certain persons in Waldington had been thinking seriously of Mr. Herbertson. Rhona, returning from Margaret Joan's birthday tea, had brought with her Mr. Herbertson's gift to that young lady. She found the Countess in the garden, for these days of brightening hope were days of broadening interest, and she had expressed a wish to visit Mr. Herbertson's greenhouse. Mrs. Hadfield, therefore, had opened the communicating door between the two gardens, and the Countess, after a wondering survey of the luxuriant scene, had sat down to rest on the Primitive Methodist garden seat beneath the cherry tree. There Rhona found her, and showed her the gift.

The Countess looked at the drawing first and then smiled over the letter. After that she turned to the drawing again, and examined it with greater care. Slowly her face lightened with recognition.

"I know this place," she said. "He has disguised it a little by these towers, so that the building might seem more of a castle to a child in this country. But it is the Castle of Zell. Of course he would have known it."

"Ah, now I remember," said Rhona. "I have seen the picture."

The Countess closed the case and restored it to its envelope. The drawing had for the moment given her a sharp thrill of pain. But she did not allow this to overcome her now. In the quiet of her refuge, with kindness about her like a protecting sea and with strength returning hour by hour, she had made the adjustments which a true woman may always be trusted to make, and to some extent at least had found peace. One of the results was an interest in those about her, new and strange though the faces were: another result was the recovery of the half-forgotten past and a quiet, ordered study of its story.

"I have been thinking to-day of Mr. Herbertson," she said. "I heard much of him once—from your father—at the time of the great desertion. He was a brilliant young man, I believe, a scholar, a master of languages. He was older than the Prince, and acquired great influence over him. Yet he did not save him.   Indeed, he was blamed most bitterly for that tragedy.   Your father, I remember, explained the failure as due to the same cause as the friendship.   There was an affinity between this man and the Prince in one thing, one secret thing which bound them together while it separated them from all other men.   And that was—Fear."

Fear?   The girl was shocked.   "You mean that they were cowards both," she cried.   "But that is impossible, Mother.   There is nothing of the coward in this man.   Consider!"

The Countess smiled.   "Have I not considered?" she said gently.   "Here in this garden I have considered it, and I think I have seen the truth.   If this man was once a coward, beloved, he has been re-made.   And we are in the place where through many years his Maker has been at work re-making a human soul; a miracle not so great as the first birth, but, next to that, the greatest in the world."

The girl did not speak.   She waited with her colour rising, her hands clasped, her eyes downcast. And her mother went on:

"This is a small place as we regard it—small and obscure and unworthy, but perhaps it was not unworthy when he came to it.   It was a garden that the Father gave to the first man He made, so the story goes.   I wonder if He gives a garden often when He desires to re-make?—sunshine and the winds, and the skies, and the rain, and the dew and the earth—all the great wonders that belong to God.   Think, too, of the training in patience, and faith, and hope, and wonder, and in the knowledge and love of beauty.   So might come the love of other beautiful things—pure thoughts and deeds, and the purest beauty of all—the soul of a little child. Do you think that cowardice and a love of beauty could exist side by side in the same heart?"

"This man is noble," whispered Rhona.

"And in the end," said the Countess, "when the hour came and the call—the call of justice, or patriotism, or pity, or love, or the appeal of a great cause—it might find him ready, his weakness gone, his heart strengthened to give to the uttermost. Yes, it is still true that a man may hide himself because he has something to conceal; but it is also true that God may hide a man—in a garden—for a great purpose."

There was silence for a moment. Then Rhona took advantage of the time and mood to ask a question which she had hesitated to ask before. It might have revealed too much of her heart.

"Do you think he has gone into great danger?"

"Our enemies will be his enemies. We know what enemies they can be. And there will be more than our own case. This man led the Prince in the matter which brought the Count into disgrace long ago. Courage was not needed then, for they both stood in the shadow of the throne; but it is a terrible thing to offend a man who will hate to the uttermost. Only young men would do it. . . . Oh, what mad things youth will do! It will play with life and death, and love and hate, and crowns and empires, before it knows what those great words mean. It plays because it does not know. Often your father woke in the night in a sweat of fear for the peril he had escaped so many years ago—the Saronio tragedy. Yet how lightly he went into it —a word, a smile, from one no wiser than himself

—a promise sealed by a glass of wine. That was all."

"And he had not escaped?"

"No. The nightmare became real at last, and killed him."

An overwhelming shadow darkened the Garden of Security. There were tears upon the mother's face.

"Oh, that madness of youth," she said. "Surely it is an understanding God who permits so much of it to be forgotten! That boy who was the cause —he was only a boy, and knew nothing; yet he dreamed that he might wear the old Iron Crown of Lusia! In after years your father often smiled at the picture—Adrian in the Iron Crown. If he had looked at the Emperor and considered the life he lived— But youth does not consider—it dreams. And he was so high in place that no one might teach him. So he played until the crash came—and then, because he was not a man at all, he failed. The pity of it! But the world has little pity to give. It seems to say that Princes have no time for play."

"You are remembering many things to-day," said Rhona compassionately.

"Yes, many. But there are more evil things than good. . . . And that is the world—"

But she checked herself. "No. That would be unjust. How can I say that, when we have come to know this man, with his garden and his books and his child friends, and these Hadfields, with their care and kindness, and that Mrs. Jenner with her loyalty and her humility and her gratitude. No, Rhona, the world is full of beauty, and the evil is only a blot upon the story.—And now, even in this maze of sorrow, I begin to see a plan."

"A plan?"

"A plan. I am sure I cannot be mistaken. And it gives the answer to your question."

Rhona waited with some wonder. With all her gentleness her mother had been a woman of great reserves, contrast and complement to her volatile and impetuous husband. But now she was deeply moved, and the reserves were broken.

"I cannot be wrong," she said. "I believe I have come back with clearer vision from the Shadow of Death. This man was given this garden, and was made anew. In the moment of need he was called out of his garden and brought to our door—the only man in England who had power to open for us the barred gates of Justice and Mercy. Was that mere chance?"

Rhona answered only by a pressure of the hand.

"So I am not afraid of our enemies now. Rather I am afraid for them. For many years God has been preparing this man to be His sword, a sword of tempered steel, slender but unbreakable. Not to avenge us only, though we may be the occasion. Our wrongs are only a part of the design. There are great events on the horizon, greater than I can measure; but the signs cannot end in a failure. No, no, it is impossible."

"I told him that he would succeed," said Rhona softly.

"You have felt it from the first. Yet he seemed so frail against those men that I feared . . . even after we came here. My fear was for you, child, not for myself. To see you in Philip's hands would be hell to me, even if you went willingly. And I dreaded lest you should become willing, at last, for my sake."

"For no other sake," murmured the girl.

"But when Mr. Herbertson spoke my fear began to pass. He seemed to understand. And when he had been to London I lost all fear. Now I have been through his garden, and have learned its purpose. He cannot fail."

If Mr. Herbertson had heard! . . . The Countess looked her daughter in the face.

"You have faith in your friend. I have faith too. Does that content you?"

The girl kissed her mother's hand before she answered:

"He has told me that he will never leave his garden, never go back to Styria."

"He does not know," said the mother gently.

Chapter XIX

The Last Day of Mr. Herbertson

HADFIELD'S night was a restless one. His mind was racked by doubt, and hovered miserably between conflicting conclusions. He went step by step through the story which Mr. Herbertson had told him on the Second of May, and tried to review everything that had happened since. He remembered one banal question of his—"What did he die of?"—and the long pause which had followed it. In the light of these recollections the Count's suggestion had a plausibility which he could not deny. Moreover, Mr. Herbertson had made no attempt to defend himself.

"Good God!" moaned Hadfield.

It was true that Count Brode had made the statement, and that it was therefore an enemy's story; but everything combined to give it weight and credibility. The old man had delighted in the young Englishman, and had taken pains to win his esteem. It was a part of his campaign, and his success was almost absolute. He had played with him, humoured him and flattered him until he had practically detached him from his principal, and had brought him into the attitude of an impartial spectator. All this would be extremely useful at the end, when the accident had occurred and would require to be explained.

Mr. Herbertson, by his very aloofness, had worked into the Count's hands, but to an extent he had now redeemed the situation by his frank appeal. Hadfield saw at last that the key to this problem was not available at present and that his course of action was clear. He must simply carry out his promise and leave the rest.

The men met as usual in the morning, and Herbertson solved an immediate difficulty. "I wish to be alone for a bit," he said. "A few things to do, you know. Suppose you take that tramp to the Red Rocks, get lunch there, and be back by tea time? You won't mind going alone, will you?"

Hadfield saw the excellence of the arrangement and accepted it gladly. As soon as he had done so, however, he perceived its purpose, and experienced some compunction. It was not strong enough to make him withdraw his acceptance—that, he saw, would be foolish under the circumstances—but it was this discomfort of mind that helped him to remember something.

"I have a letter for you," he said, "a large letter addressed in a sufficiently large handwriting. It was entrusted to me to give to you on a certain birthday."

"Margaret Joan's, of course," said Mr. Herbertson. "Yes, I shall be glad to have it."

Hadfield produced the packet, which was certainly addressed with sufficient emphasis in a quite familiar hand. Mr. Herbertson took it with a smile, but did not open it at the time. He waited until Hadfield had gone and he was alone in a retreat which he had discovered among the rocks.

As he had expected, the packet contained a photograph of Margaret Joan, specially taken for this eighth birthday, a very excellent sketch-portrait from which the child looked at him with that quizzical, half-mischievous expression which she usually wore when he embarked upon one of his make-believe efforts. "Are you forgetting that I am now quite grown up, Mr. Herbertson?" she said now, as plainly as though in words; and the man who had known every change on that innocent face thrilled with pleasure to see that look once more. When he had said good-bye he had realised that he would never see her again, but in his darkest hour Margaret Joan had refused to be left behind. And the inscription on the back of the card was brief but comprehensive: "To my Chumm with all my heart."

It was some time before Mr. Herbertson restored the welcome photograph to its envelope and laid them aside. He would not go back to Waldington to Margaret Joan. If he went back now he could never again look the child in the eyes: but because he was here at Saint Claud on his dire errand he could accept her love. "Which is a curious paradox," he decided. "It will only be by losing her that I shall keep her. Another ancient problem for the youthful curate at St. Augustine's!"

He decided that he would give the morning to Margaret, whatever the evening might bring. "And I have to thank her for a last joyous occupation," he reflected. "She shall have such a letter as a little maid of eight never received before." Behold, then, Mr. Herbertson spending the last morning of his life in writing a long letter to a child; writing it, too, with the care which he always gave to his essays. It was the last, and it must be the best.

When this was done he went back to lunch at the Seine, and as Hadfield was not there he chose a seat adjacent to a table where a shop-keeper of Dieppe sat with his wife and child. He had already made this little maid's acquaintance, and now he renewed the acquaintance and extended it to the parents. In a short time relations were so easy that it became possible for him to make the suggestion which had been in his mind from the first. He was going into Tréport in the afternoon in an open carriage, and it would please him much if he might have the company of Denise. They would call at a bookseller's in the town, where he felt sure he could find a gift that would please her; and they would be back in good time, as he had an appointment with his friends in the evening. So declared Mr. Herbertson, with as much deference as if Denise had been a young countess instead of the very young daughter of a draper of Dieppe; and so happy was the impression he made upon the mother of Denise that his request was granted with an ocean of smiles. The mother took the child to dress, and half-an-hour later the adventurers set out, to spend an afternoon which one of them will remember with joy when thousands of other afternoons have been forgotten.

The return took place as arranged, one of the pair coming home laden with gifts and quivering with delight, the other convinced that he could not have spent his last afternoon to better purpose.

He had been enabled to forget for a time. Now he was obliged to remember, but it would have required a very observant person to detect any signs of a troubled heart in his demeanour.

Hadfield returned soon after, and a little business was necessary at that point; but though Mr. Herbertson had to convey an impression of great earnestness in this matter, he succeeded in carrying it through without creating any inconvenient uneasiness in his friend's mind. The conversation took place in his own room.

"As you know, Hadfield," he said, "no sensible man takes a risk without making certain arrangements. Accidents are always possible, even in a duel!"

Hadfield smiled and nodded. He remembered the methodical habits of his neighbour. Mr. Herbertson produced two sealed envelopes which, curiously enough, he had kept about his person since he had prepared them.

"One," he said, "is addressed to yourself, as you see. It tells you how you should act in the event of such an accident. This other, which bears no address at all, contains a telegram, which must be despatched at the earliest possible moment afterwards—as soon as you can reach a telegraph station. There must be no failure in this."

He spoke so gravely that Hadfield was alarmed. Mr. Herbertson saw the look—that open, boyish face told its story so clearly!

"Oh," he said, smiling, "don't be over-impressed. This is all for your guidance in an extreme case."

"Then, of course," said Hadfield, "when it is all over I shall give them back to you."

"Precisely. But I want you to remember that in the unlikely event of an accident you are to use them as I have stated. Moreover, you will not give the Count any inkling of their existence. It is a matter for your own hands."

It was very difficult to speak with sufficient gravity to impress his hearer and at the same time to preserve the make-believe atmosphere which was so necessary to the plot. Looking into Hadfield's bewildered face, Herbertson realised again the slenderness of the thread on which his hopes hung; here the good faith of a young fellow who was practically blindfold and, if anything, suspicious of him; there the whim of an old man who had taken care to promise nothing.

The realisation was unnerving, so he fought it aside. "Here are the packets," he said; "fasten them up in your breast-pocket—so. And now we will keep our appointment."

He gave one look around the room. As far as he knew, all was in order, and he had left no possibility of uncertainty or confusion. If it had been an ordinary man the preparations would have seemed suspiciously complete; but here on the spot was Hadfield, to testify to his neighbour's ridiculous passion for order and method.

They took the winding cliff path which led to the sands. At the foot a turn to the left would have taken them safely, inside the shelter of the cliff, around to the road leading to the railway station. If Mr. Herbertson felt temptation at that point it was sharp and short, for in three or four minutes they were clear of the cliff and crossing the sands towards the appointed place. He knew that his enemy was watching that walk from one of the windows of the hotel, and wondered what he was thinking at this juncture. Doubtless his triumph was mingled with a little surprise. At all events, in his hate he had given his victim a life's opportunity. He prayed fervently that the victim might be man enough to work it out!

The walk was a very brief one, and almost silent. It seemed to him only a little while before they were passing between the great boulders which marked the end of his pilgrimage, Hadfield leading the way. The rocks were scattered and irregular, and the sand lay between them in broad beaten pathways. In one place they opened out into a kind of rude amphitheatre, with paths leading away in different directions. This was where the pistol practice had taken place and where the duel was to be fought.

"It's an ideal spot," said Hadfield. "No one can see what goes on until he comes quite close. And, of course, we should keep a look-out."

Mr. Herbertson agreed that the spot was ideal for their purpose. It was something vaguely like a gigantic rat-trap. After examining the place he sat down upon a flat, smooth-faced piece of rock to wait.

"It will be half-an-hour at least," said Hadfield. "We can't expect them before that. What shall we do?"

He experienced a little boyish excitement. Forgetting the shadow between them, he stood discussing the probable arrangements.

"I suppose it will be just one shot," he said. "At a certain number of paces. Or would it be in the old American style—back to back, and then turn to fire? Which would you prefer?"

"I am quite unbiased," replied Mr. Herbertson listlessly. "I think we may leave that to the other party. I fall in, of course, with any arrangement you may come to."

"Then the Count will decide?"

"Yes. I think we may safely leave it to him."

"Very good. Now I think I'll go to the opening, and keep a look-out."

Mr. Herbertson agreed with some relief. This talk irked him. So Hadfield left the ground and mounted one of the scattered rocks outside, where he could enjoy a view of the sands up to the base of the cliff on which the hotel stood.

So far there was no one in sight—no one of the description he looked for. The sands they had crossed were clear, and even beyond, near the village, there were only two or three children playing at the water-side.

As no particular time had been fixed, they might have to wait an hour. Presently he thought he would go back and speak to Herbertson; so back he went, treading softly on the sand. But when he reached the place he saw that Mr. Herbertson was sitting in the same spot, with his face buried in his hands. Then it did somehow occur to Hadfield that the man might really prefer to be alone, and after all it was rather difficult to carry on conversation with that unsolved problem between them. "I won't disturb him," he thought, "until they're in sight." So he returned to his perch.

Still the way across the sands was deserted, and no one issued from under the cliff; but there were a few more children over yonder, and one or two older people among them.

Soon afterwards he thought that their plan would suffer interference. There was a pretty farmhouse in a field behind the beach a little farther down, and from this direction came an old gentleman, evidently a visitor. He walked slowly along above the rocks, as if he intended to locate himself somewhere among them; but this was not his purpose, for presently he skirted them and moved away down towards the sea. He was a careful old gentleman, for he wore a plentiful white handkerchief behind his straw hat to keep off the sun; and he carried a newspaper, neatly folded, under his arm. He held on his way down to the water's edge, where he soon found a seat which he had probably used before. When he sat down he was just out of sight, though Hadfield saw the corner of his newspaper as he opened it to read. This old gentleman would presently hear pistol shots, but as he was quite a distance away they would scarcely disturb him. Besides, he had doubtless heard such sounds before.

Again he turned his eyes towards the hotel.

.   .   .   .

Mr. Herbertson, sitting with his face in his hands, could shut out the streaming sunshine, the voice of the sea, but he could not forget; and as he could not forget he tried to keep one clear issue before him. His thoughts might wander, but he always brought them back to this: Restitution!

It was not yet too late, for the open country was before him. But he shut out this idea, just as he tried to shut out the sunshine. He endeavoured, instead, to recall the face of the woman whom he had told to pray for him. She had promised to do so, and she had certainly done so. Perhaps that was why he was here now! Then he recalled that incident from her girlhood. How strange that she should have told it! But since she had told it, he must certainly stay here to be killed. He could not attempt to escape.

At that moment Hadfield appeared at the entrance to the amphitheatre.

"They are coming," he cried. "They have just left the hotel."

Mr. Herbertson looked up and nodded. Hadfield, after a moment's hesitation, returned slowly to his observatory.

Chapter XX

Count Brode Arranges to Drop a Handkerchief

LEFT alone, Mr. Herbertson remained sitting for a little longer. He had a confused desire to go over the whole argument again, so that he might prove to his last satisfaction that he was doing the right thing and the best thing. Could a man never, never travel far enough to outride his own doubt, his self-distrust? These curses that accompanied him to the edge of the grave—would they pursue him after? Ah, James, James, you will be a futile person to the very end!

With bitter self-scorn he realised that there was no time to argue now. He heard voices, and rose.

"You thought we were not coming," said the Count, as Hadfield advanced to meet them. "My dear sir, how could we fail? It was, I assure you, impossible! And Mr. Herbertson—is he impatient? He, at least, knew that we would come!"

"He has been resting," said Hadfield innocently, and a little embarrassed. When this old man spoke he made everything so smooth that suspicion seemed to be a sin. "Ah, here he is."

Herbertson came out to meet them. "I leave everything to you, Hadfield," he said a little abruptly. "Only, don't be too long. We may be interrupted at any moment."

Hadfield received the instruction with a little surprise, but at once turned to Count Brode. "I am not an expert in these matters," he said. "Perhaps you have a suggestion to make as to the arrangements."

The Count's urbanity was something to study. Possibly it increased in the same ratio as his hatred. The morning, the whole day, had tried him severely, and when he had seen Mr. Herbertson set out for the rendezvous his rage and chagrin had reached a climax. At that point he had been obliged to abandon many plausible suppositions and to fall back upon what seemed the only explanation.

"The fool!" he had said. "He is trusting to my fear. He thinks I will not dare to do it. He does not know me!"

Then he addressed Philip, skilfully disguising his discomfiture.

"I did not believe," he said carelessly, "that the fellow would face you. I doubt it even now. If he does, it will be because he thinks you will not kill."

Philip, examining his revolvers, gave a brief answer. He was sick of these people, these surroundings, and this mystery. "We will assure him," he said sullenly.

"Just so. Do it thoroughly, Philip. At the same time, give him, say, a few moments after the shot—to compose his mind."

There was a pause. Then the son made a lame but honest attempt to clear things up.

"I hate these mysteries," he said. "Why will you

not speak out? I will not shoot any the less well."

Count Brode longed to speak. It would have relieved his mind so much, but he believed that his wisdom was stronger than his longing. All through his life, indeed, he had studied the art of making wisdom rule all other considerations. He did not know that this power had left him, and he did not realise that the younger man was in a very dangerous temper.

"My dear Philip, you have not long to wait. And it will be a better story then. Trust me." And to himself he muttered, "Where there is no knowledge there is no guilt."

So he had refused to speak, and they had set out together for the meeting-place—the son sullen but inflamed, the father using all his power of will to hide his excitement and passion. In the hall below the cases had been handed to a boy who was waiting for them; but when they were near the rocks the boy had been sent back upon an errand calculated to delay him considerably. Then they had proceeded alone; and as they approached the rocks the Count's anticipation became so keen that it obscured once more the truth which had been trying to suggest itself to his mind for some time— that whether he played on or abandoned his purpose, he was a beaten player. Hate had stifled reason, blinded cunning, silenced prudence, for where it is allowed to reign it tolerates no rival.

"My dear Mr. Hadfield," he said now, "I am delighted to place my little experience at your disposal. I have been thinking of an arrangement which may be satisfactory. Shall I describe it?"

"Please do," said Hadfield.

"This arena of ours, then, measures some thirty paces across. I propose that our principals shall stand twenty paces apart or so—rather more, you will observe, than is usual. They shall stand with hands at their sides until a signal is given, then fire one shot simultaneously. Will that do?"

"It sounds very simple," said Hadfield; and he added further: "It seems to me a very good arrangement. And the signal?"

"One of us shall drop a handkerchief. And I should like you, Mr. Hadfield, to undertake that office—for your friend's satisfaction."

Hadfield had not anticipated this. After the first surprise he felt a little flattered, but a little disturbed at the idea of responsibility. Great was his astonishment when Mr. Herbertson intervened.

"One moment," he said nervously. "I do not wish to interfere, but—but that must not be. Hadfield, you must not undertake it. Let the Count carry out all the arrangements himself."

In the manner, as well as in the words, the note of urgency was clear. Count Brode saw that it must be smoothed away. He was baulked of one refinement of his plot—almost a master-stroke, indeed—but it was better to let this go. There must be no scene. Indeed, he could afford to let it go, for that outbreak suggested great distress of mind in the one who had made it. He bowed and smiled in instant agreement.

"As you please, of course, Mr. Herbertson. At your request I shall be charmed to drop the handkerchief."

The remaining arrangements were rapidly completed. Philip chose a revolver, and the Count

handed another to Mr. Herbertson. "Mr. Hadfield
will doubtless examine it for you," he murmured;
and Hadfield proceeded to do so. Afterwards he
gave it back to Mr. Herbertson with some word of
assurance. At the same moment he wondered
vaguely whether the man knew how to fire it. But
of course he did not mean to fire it. Then the two
principals were facing each other at a distance of
some twenty paces across the sand. On the one
side was the Count, stepping backwards to his place
with a handkerchief in his hand. On the other
side Hadfield was standing against a boulder of rock.

At this point the young man discovered that he
was greatly agitated—that he was waiting breathlessly, with his heart in his throat. At the same
time his eyes began to torment him with disturbing
hallucinations. He saw in the face of Mr. Herbertson what he had never seen in any face before—
a drawn greyness which was terrible. Was it—
could it be—what people vaguely called the Shadow
of Death? Then, struggling with that horrible
thought, he glanced at Philip Brode; and after that
glance he knew that if he had had the courage at
that crisis to do his plain duty he would have shouted
"Murder!" And yet—and yet there was something so unreal about the whole affair that in the
same moment he was blaming himself for his own
agitation.

The Count had found his place. He stood perfectly still, extending his right hand with the handkerchief. He did not once glance at his son, but
kept his eyes upon Mr. Herbertson. He looked
and waited, enjoying what should have been the
sweetest moments of his life. Perhaps they were,

but they were very brief. The opponents stood motionless, Mr. Herbertson grey and rigid, his enemy relaxed but ready. Then the Count turned his eyes upon Hadfield, as though seeking his assent; and at the same instant a man emerged from among the rocks behind Hadfield and stood at that young man's elbow.

This man had calculated his distance exactly, and in fact had rehearsed this appearance; but it was mere accident that the first to see him should have been the arch-schemer. The old man stood in the same position, with the outstretched hand, the suspended signal, but his smile made grotesque and foolish by sudden, overwhelming dismay. To him the apparition was not merely interruption— it was much more even than the bitterness of frustration and defeat. He saw himself bound and delivered, set in a cleft from which there was no escape. That strong, emotionless face was Judgment, Disaster, Doom.

So the pause was lengthened. Then Hadfield saw the Count's face, and knew that something had happened. Immediately he was aware of a presence at his side. He turned, and Philip turned at the same time.

They saw a middle-aged gentleman in grey, a masterful and self-possessed person who looked upon the tableau with a certain appreciation. He was the man whom Hadfield had seen making his way to the waterside some time before. But he was not nearly so old a person as he had seemed from a distance. Indeed, Hadfield could hardly believe that it was the same man. But there was the hat and the handkerchief.

Count Brode made one hopeless effort to escape. "There, Philip, that will do," he cried lightly. "The play is over. You timed yourself very well, Baron."

Ronnefeldt did not answer. His silence was contempt immeasurable. But in a moment his eyes left the Count and turned to another actor in the drama. Then he pointed with his cane.

Mr. Herbertson had broken down. The weak man had borne a tremendous strain. At the last moment he had awakened to a full consciousness of what was doing, and had suffered as much as even Count Brode could have desired. His heart had become a shrinking, tortured creature in a cage, his body a mass of nerves in torment. He had awaited in horrible suspense the crash of the bullet, and had wondered that he could still stand upright. All this was the agony which men call Death, the price that must be paid for Remission. . . . And in the midst of that torture came a glimpse of a long, narrow garden, and a grey framework rising between the branches of cherry trees, and a woman looking up at it. . . .

Then he had heard a voice—Brode's voice—and the present world had come back in a fierce glimpse of sand and rock and sky and faces. But there was one face which had not been there before; and when he had perceived this, his will had snapped. The pistol dropped from his hand, he swayed backwards, clutched at the rough rock, and sank down at its base. And as he sank he gave a shuddering sob.

They all heard it, and Hadfield ran over to him.

The Count made two steps in the same direction, speaking as he moved.

"I assure you, Ronnefeldt," he said, with all the art of which he was master, "it is all a—"

But the Baron took no notice of the unfinished appeal. He seemed to wave it away contemptuously, walked over to the prostrate man, and knelt down at his side. Discomfited, dazed, despairing, the Count turned back to his son.

The others never really knew what passed between the two. It was easy to surmise that Philip's passion had been steadily increasing during those last moments. In the new development he had seen himself robbed of his victim, but that was not all. The players in this game of mystery had ignored him, had swept him aside without a word or a thought. Perhaps the conviction had come that he had been used as an instrument only, not intelligent enough to be taken behind the scenes, only useful to work out the deep schemes of the old man whose ability had often been an oppression to be dumbly resented. Moreover, he had been drinking, and one spark of anger was enough to provoke a conflagration.

There were a few indistinct sentences, full of choking rage on the one side, of assurance and persuasion on the other. Then Philip's voice rose in a shout:

"Stand back! You shall not fool me again. Let me pass. I will kill him!"

Hadfield looked up at the sound of danger. He saw Philip striding down upon them, the revolver still in his hand, his face crimson with rage, distorted by mortification. Then he saw the Count spring upon him from behind, seizing his arm; and at the same instant Ronnefeldt, with a swift movement, picked up the weapon which Mr. Herbertson had dropped.

"Philip!" cried the Count. "Wait—listen—I speak to you—"

But there was no time for reason; and even if he had been able to speak the truth at that moment it would have been in vain. That old hate would have required so much explanation. The arm he had seized was torn away from his grasp. Instantly he seized it again, and the contact became a swift, hot struggle, the man fighting to hold the beast. In the struggle they bent over the pistol. Suddenly a dull report rang out, the two struggling figures parted, and one of them reeled to the ground.

Hadfield gasped "Good God!" Nevertheless he could not believe that it was really a tragedy. It was some hideous illusion.

It was the older man who had fallen. They saw Philip stand over him, dazed but tragically sobered. He seemed to wait in a terrible hush for his father to move or speak: and there was some movement, but not the movement of life. Then he bent over the extended form, and saw what they all saw later—a small wound under the chin, where the bullet had passed up to the brain.

Philip stood upright. After a moment he raised his eyes from that ghastly heap, and brushed his hand across his face. Then, doubtless, realisation came, piercing the haze of wine and passion, paralysing his heart with an indescribable horror. He shuddered. Then he became aware of the weapon in his hand, looked round, and saw his enemies. They were as silent, as motionless, as the rocks about them, but he did not follow his first intention and seek to turn the amphitheatre into a madman's shambles. He was not checked by the sight of Ronnefeldt's face, white with emotion but immovably resolute. What came to him was the realisation that even if he killed them all he he could not undo that deed. Indescribable, unspeakable, it was for ever. He groaned; and in that paroxysm of horror he was stung to the noblest impulse, perhaps, of his wayward manhood, the one response that he could make to the dead man's cruel affection. For he sank on his knees beside his father's body, and raised the revolver to his own head.

"O God!" stammered Hadfield.

Philip fired.

Directly afterwards a man came into the arena. It was the young Swiss waiter from the hotel, who had been so attentive to the party of guests. He had been hidden just out of sight, and the shots had brought him forward. When he saw what had happened he stood transfixed. The Baron spoke sharply, and he hastened away for assistance. But he did not go to the hotel. He went towards the farm.

Presently Hadfield found that he was being addressed in English. "Be yourself, sir," said the Baron. "Your companion needs you. Do not look more at those."

The whole horror had occupied less than a minute. Mr. Herbertson was still lying in a swoon. Less than a minute! Up to now Hadfield's course had lain in quiet ways.

"He is dead too," he muttered, with a shudder.

"No. He has only fainted. A little way down that path by which I came you will find a pool of water. Dip your handkerchief, and bring it to me."

Hadfield obeyed blindly. Somehow he found the water, somehow carried out his instructions. As he did so he wondered how this person could do such trivial things in the face of tragedy—could so carefully lave a fainting man's face while two others lay dead within twenty paces. Some indignation mingled with his wonder.

Then the story opened out before him, the key was placed in his hand. Consciousness was reluctant to return, but in a while the grey face seemed to relax. Then the Baron, bending lower, addressed Mr. Herbertson by a name which Hadfield heard in a mist of bewilderment.

"What did you say?" he asked, scarcely knowing that he spoke at all.

Ronnefeldt looked up. There was no longer need for concealment.

"You have known him as James Herbertson," he said. "But it was James Herbertson that died twelve years ago, in London. This man was once, and is again to-day, Adrian Zenandra, Prince of Zell!"

Chapter XXI

The Prince of Zell Walks in Another Garden

LIFE at Waldington had fallen back into its ordinary channels for sometime. Hadfield had succumbed again to the routine of the office, and was as regular as ever in his departure from the house in the morning and his return to it for lunch and rest. There were, however, certain signs which a few people marked with sympathy or amusement according to their own dispositions. For instance, he never passed Mr. Herbertson's house without looking up to the empty windows to see that all was well with it, and he never went to rest at night without making a tour of inspection in Mr. Herbertson's tangled garden. Further, instead of patronising the irresponsible press of a morning he would take the *Daily Telegraph* or *The Times* instead; and it was understood that he did this because he was greatly interested in Continental politics.

A day in October brought important events. By the morning post came a solicitor's letter which had been expected for some time, and as a consequence Hadfield went out of his house that day in a state of exhilaration. Further, when he opened his *Telegraph* one of the first things he saw was the name of Styria, in heavy capitals, and before he reached the office he had read what is now familiar history—the introduction into the House of Assembly of the Chancellor Ronnefeldt's Bill for the new Lusian Constitution, and its adoption by a great majority. When he had read the report of the news agency he turned to another column for the Graaden Letter; and there he found a couple of paragraphs which he read with vivid interest and delight:

"Naturally," wrote the Graaden gossip, "the only topic here is the new Lusian Constitution, and the Chancellor's triumph. Undoubtedly history has been written within these last days, but there is one aspect of the subject which gives a romantic interest to this great political venture. It has been rumoured for some days that an exile of very high rank, who was supposed to have died abroad some years ago, had mysteriously reappeared and had been restored to the Emperor's favour. Even now I am not permitted to give the name, but it is one which the Irreconcilables have used without stint as a weapon in their quarrel with the Imperial Party. They absolutely refused to credit the rumours I have mentioned, and were dumbfounded when on the introduction of the Bill the returned exile was seen in the Royal Gallery with the Archduke Ernest. At this opportune moment a question from one of his own supporters enabled the Chancellor to announce not only the return and reconciliation, but also the fact that by the distinguished exile's intercession several other prominent refugees had been pardoned and restored.

"When the announcement was made the

enthusiasm was extraordinary. The Emperor was wildly cheered, and for once the Irreconcilables became a negligible quantity. Indeed, it may be claimed that this diversion ensured the adoption of the Bill in an atmosphere entirely beyond expectation.

"The particulars of the affair are involved in mystery, but as the personage in question is now staying at the palace there can be no doubt as to the fact of the reconciliation. There must have been many obstacles in the way, and the gossips make the most amazing statements in their search for an explanation. It is generally considered that the Imperial Chancellor had some share in the matter, but he stands so high in the general esteem that even his opponents would not suggest any intrigue on his part. It would probably be felt that he deserved any fortunate accident that might aid his purposes; and certainly no more dramatic incident could have been provided to illustrate the absolute goodwill of the Throne."

Hadfield read these paragraphs several times, and felt that he could have given supplementary information of a valuable kind. At eleven he went out to call upon the solicitor whose letter had reached him that morning, and at one he was on his way home to lunch, taking with him the *Daily Telegraph* and a trifling article which he had purchased at a stationer's.

His wife received him with the smile which Mr. Herbertson had learned to appreciate in the earlier days.

"Well," she asked eagerly, "is it all settled?"

"Yes, old thing," he replied. "It is all settled.

And we can look for a tenant. But first I want to show you something in to-day's paper."

So Mrs. Hadfield also read the gossip from Styria, and read it with full understanding of those particulars which did not appear in print. And when they had discussed it briefly they proceeded to the moral, Hadfield producing the trifling article which he had purchased on the way home. It was a small sheet containing the legend, "This House to Let." Sitting down at the table he wrote at the foot of the paper, with pardonable pride: "Apply to the owner, No. 6."

"We'll go," he said, when this was done, "and put it up now."

He took a key from the sideboard, and they went together to the house which had been the home of Mr. Herbertson for so many years. The door gave out an unfamiliar hollow sound when the key was placed in the lock, and when they entered the hall their steps called desolate echoes from the swept and empty chambers. The contents, except those few things which the Prince had wished to have or had given to the delighted Mrs. Jenner, and those which Hadfield had selected as mementoes, had been sold, the books and the papers had been packed away to Graaden, and to-day Hadfield had seen the deed of gift by which the pleasant little property had become theirs. And now there was nothing to show what kind of tenant the last had been, or to suggest the curious secret which the walls had sheltered during those long days.

After much consideration the Hadfields had decided, plain commonsense over-ruling sentiment in this particular, that it would be better to let the house than to live in it themselves; the garden would be a valuable attraction to a tenant of Mr. Herbertson's tastes, and Hadfield had no inclination to undertake it. Indeed, when he looked at that over-luxuriant domain and its unfinished *magnum opus* he felt that his quondam neighbour had exhibited signs of greatness which no one had recognised. Only a man of the true Imperial spirit could have set himself such a task!

In the front window downstairs they placed the notice they had brought. Perhaps it was the fittest thing in the world that they should have placed it there; for that notice was the *Finis* to a tale of reproach, and that room had seen many phases of the battle by which Mr. Herbertson had won through to write that word and to begin a new story in a higher place.

When they had done this they went through the house to survey it as their own possession, so artless and childlike they were, this young Englishman and his bride. Presently they came to the room overlooking the garden, the room in which Mr. Herbertson had been accustomed to write his essays. It was now a bare room from which the soul had gone, and yet it was the one room in which a memento remained. This lay face downwards on the mantelpiece.

"Why, look at this," said Hadfield. "It is his calendar!"

It was, indeed, Mr. Herbertson's Shakespeare Calendar, soiled and dusty but rescued from the floor by a conscientious charwoman. When they examined it they saw through the dust the broad, domed forehead of the Bard of Humanity, and the eyes full of that patient wisdom that can await fulfilments. And on the slip they read the last quotation that Mr. Herbertson had turned up:

TUESDAY

2

MAY

"Things base and vile, holding no quantity,
 Love can transpose to form and dignity;
 Love looks not with the eyes but with the mind,
 And therefore is winged Cupid painted blind."

"Why," said Hadfield, "that was the day it all began, you know. And somehow he never turned another page after that. Perhaps he had too much to think of. But anyway I don't see that the lines suited the day very well, as far as he was concerned. If there was one thing he would have nothing to do with, it was love. Why, never in my life did I hear him talk about women. They were out of his scheme entirely."

His wife stood looking at the quotation, something indefinable in the bright eyes under their dark lashes. It had to do with thoughts which she would never reveal to any living soul.

"You are quite sure?" she said suddenly. "Are there really any men like that?"

Hadfield considered. "Oh, well," he said, "of course there shouldn't be. But if there is such a man, I fancy he lived in this house!"

That was final, though the Bard still wore that look of patient wisdom. "We'll go upstairs now," said Hadfield, replacing the calendar upon the mantelpiece. "But we must remember to take this away with us when we come down." And when they did return the new owner of the house took the calendar with him. Later it reappeared on his walnut sideboard, neatly framed to protect it from the dust, and its message fully justified by events; and there you may find it still, a constant reminder of a very remarkable romance and of the magnificent transformations of love.

On that day the Prince of Zell took a walk in the Palace gardens at Graaden.

Our Mr. Herbertson was now convalescent, but far from a condition in which he would be able to face the calls of his new life. Those tense days of May and early June had ended in an illness which seemed reluctant to release him. After the tragic encounter he had been taken to the farm where Ronnefeldt had lodged, and had spent some weeks on the very brink of the river of death. The over-strained system had collapsed, and the physician and nurses from Dieppe had found him a problem which baffled all their care and skill. While their patient was awake he lay listless and apparently hopeless, but they felt that if that had been the worst his recovery might have been only a matter of time. In the night, however, all their work was undone, for when guardian consciousness had left her post the legions of pain made this frail being their prey. He had been forced to bear anew all the secret agonies of twenty years. He had stood before the pistol in the sandy amphitheatre, had cowered before his tormentor in the Petersburg, had sought to climb in anguish a precipice which had no summit. He had stood at the door of Ronnefeldt's house, but a door that would not open, and sometimes in the summer-house in the Palace gardens, pleading to a man of stone. Sometimes he had struggled in the slough of his own doubts and fears, leaving blood in every footprint; but the greatest torture of all had come in re-living the black hours of his fall, when he had chosen the path of shame. Then, sometimes in a moan, sometimes in a cry that had torn the silence of the night and startled the sleepers in distant chambers, he had echoed that stark despair. "I cannot face him, I cannot face him! Herbertson, I cannot face him!"

Hadfield, of course, had returned to Waldington, content at leaving his friend in good hands and eager to tell his amazing story to the others. After sending letters, which had perforce been left unopened, they had rested in patient expectation, ignorant of the truth. Ronnefeldt was at that time the busiest man in Europe, but it was he that had averted a fatal issue. Alarmed by the medical report he had gone down to Saint Claud, and having spent a night there had returned to Graaden to tell his story. Nor had it been told in vain, for at dawn next morning an old man had set out for the farm by the sea.

He had gone in his accustomed silence, the silence in which he had received those blows which had made his reign a splendid tragedy; but he had gone as the eagle goes, with mighty speed and direct to his goal. The great Trans-Continental trains waited to let him pass, their occupants wondering what fateful call had brought him out. All things were made easy, as they always were when the Eagle went abroad, until he sat by the bed of the man who had wronged him so grievously long ago. The Prince, dozing with drawn cheeks and furrowed brows, had not opened his eyes, supposing his visitor to be one of his nurses; but as the moments passed some consciousness had come to him, and he seemed to listen, breathless; but before he could open his eyes a hand had taken his, and a voice had spoken:

"My boy!"

Much may be said in a phrase, more in a look if there are tears in the eyes; but the great fact was that the old man had come! No one else ever knew what other words had passed, but when the visitor left an hour later the legions of torment had been routed. From that day the invalid had made progress, had turned his face to the window instead of to the wall, and had known the balm of quiet sleep. In a month he had been able to travel by stages to Styria, to make his home for the time in the Palace. Then he had been able to attend to correspondence and to see friends, until, last night, he had faced the last ordeal of his return and his atonement by appearing in the Assembly.

Now he could see it all again—the crimson benches that gradually filled with crowding forms, the faces that seemed all alike to the man who sat tense but half-fainting in the Imperial gallery, the sudden hush that seemed to spread over the excited House as the tidings passed from one to another; then the stir of whispers, the long, intent stare from hundreds of eyes, the wonder, the silence, the sensation as they gazed upon the man who had come to meet his accumulation of shame. And for hours he had sat grimly before those eyes, drinking his cup of confusion to the dregs, leaving only when he had known that his work was done.

Now that ordeal was over too, and it was once more a sunny morning in a garden, though an autumn morning and another garden. He had looked at an avalanche of letters and telegrams before coming out, most of them from men and women in the capital who were eager to welcome him back to his place. He had opened only a few of these, and had then selected two which had come from England. One was from Hadfield, delightfully cordial but curiously stilted, for poor Hadfield could not find a phraseology which would serve at the same time for the Herbertson of his heart and the Serene Highness of the recent revelation. He gave a few details of the disposition of the "furniture and effects" of Number Four Arran Terrace, which had been completed last week, and went on to say that it was very quiet in the Terrace since his neighbours had left it. "But I hope you are making satisfactory progress, and we cannot find words (at least I can't, though perhaps Mrs. H. can) to express our deep appreciation of Your Highness's kindness. As for Mrs. Jenner, happy for life on her pension, she has plenty of words, though many of them get swamped in tears of joy. She has just been here to tell us of the pleasant little home she has set up, where she will board and lodge two gentlemen in the hope of ultimately coming upon another prince among her boarders, and where Apple Dumplings will be a frequent feature of the menu. As for Your Highness's garden, I keep it in order as far as I can myself, and also have a man in to help. It shan't go to the wild, not if I know it, and I confidently hope to find a tenant who will value the garden and finish the greenhouse. And we all send our respectful love and good wishes."

The other letter, addressed in a hand quite familiar to the recipient, had been charged excess postage by a vigilant office which had seen to its safe delivery in order that the excess might be secured. Not that it should have gone astray in any case, despite Margaret's punctuation and spelling.

Mr. Prince of Zell
The Emperor's Pallace,
Styrrier. Europe.

All was in pencil, for the letter had been written semi-surreptitiously.

My Dearest Prince,

I hope you are quite well now. I hope you won't mind my writing. Daddy said it wouldent be wise to write till you ask me too but is that true and arnt you my best friend any longer. Cant people be friends if one of them is a prince. Mummy thinks it almost impossible but I said Id ask you and she said Id better and I said I would and she said yes. She doesent no Im writing but she did say yes so thats that. O dear Mr.—I mean Prince—cant we still be chums. I dont know what I shall do without you and can we put crosses in a letter to a prince.

Your ever loving friend,
Margaret Joan Mead.

These were voices from the garden, faint for the distance, but sweet and friendly. They warmed him as the sun warmed the fresh autumn air of

the morning. Margaret should have her answer
—he would write it to-day. Meanwhile—

Meanwhile here was Ronnefeldt, striding up the
broad walk, strong in health and confidence, with
the smile of a friend and the hand-clasp of a giant.
"I am glad you are out," he cried. "I feared that
you might be tired after last evening. I have come
to thank you."

"You—to thank me?" cried the Prince.

"Why, yes. I am most heavily in your debt.
We are all in your debt."

The Prince was confused, as though an uncon-
sidered point of view had been presented too
suddenly. He laughed and flushed.

"Oh, no," he protested. "There spoke an
enthusiast—and a friend. But let me take your
arm, and we will go over to that summer-house."

They went together, slowly. "Oh, but I mean
it," said Ronnefeldt, earnestly. "I do not say that
the Measure would not have been well received.
But it was triumphant beyond all hope, and that
was largely due to you. And because I can imagine
what it cost you, I have come to say 'Thank you!'"

"Ah, well," said the Prince. "It is good to find
a friend so generous. Some of us have better
reason for gratitude, and we say less. . . . Yes, it
cost me something, but I owed much more and had
no more to give."

"There will be call for more in the days to come,
Adrian, and you will give it. For all those years,
in spite of all, I have had that hope for you."

"What?" cried the Prince. "You knew?"

"I knew. No one else, not even he. While you
lived I kept in touch, and I did not lose touch

when you seemed to die. But how little a man may be able to do for his friend through twenty years! I could not stir a finger for you, for your way was best. Whatever was done must be done by you alone. Even when you came at last I was afraid—afraid."

They came to the summer-house. The Prince sat down, already tired, and Ronnefeldt stood at the door.

"You had reason to be afraid," said the Prince; and he thought of the battle so often lost, so hardly won, the black fight through which Margaret Joan flitted like an Ariel and Rhona shone like a goddess. At the thought came shame, burning shame, and self-scorn. "Ah, yes, you had reason to be afraid. And I feel that it would be better, far better, if I could go back. Not there, of course, but to some such life as that. I am not equal to this."

Ronnefeldt pondered, with some wonder in his eyes. "But, my dear Adrian," he said, "if you were able to face what you have already faced, you need not fear anything in the future."

From the Prince's expression it was clear that this, too, was a new and surprising aspect of the situation. A moment's thought, however, gave him an answer.

"Ah," he said. "You appraise that much too highly. I—I could not refuse. There were certain factors present—"

What need to explain what those factors had been? Ronnefeldt waited, still with that look of wonder. The Prince ended lamely:

"Certain factors which will not be present in the future."

"Will they not?"

The Prince shook his head. There was a long pause, while the Baron wondered how far this man's humility and self-scorn would take him. It would take a man nowhere, he decided quickly. It would mean disaster and frustration to the end. There was deep earnestness, therefore, in his next words.

"Let the past be buried, Adrian. You are called to a new life . . . clearly called, I believe. And I beg of you this—that when happiness offers itself, as it certainly will, you will let no influence of the past hinder you from taking it."

What did he mean? The Prince was puzzled, but he had no time to ask a question. A young man came up the broad path which led down towards the White House. Ronnefeldt went a couple of paces to meet him to receive his message.

"Rudolf?" murmured the Prince, incredulously.

"I am glad to see your Highness so much better," said Rudolf, smiling; and Ronnefeldt explained: "Rudolf," he said, "is a confidential helper loaned to me by the Secret Service Department. He is excellent as a waiter, and good in many other vocations. He tells me that callers have arrived and are awaiting me. Shall we leave you here?"

"For half an hour or so," said the Prince. "My servant will come for me presently. I am obliged to you for all your good counsel."

"Be obliged, if you please," said the Baron, "but above all be obedient. Especially to my last piece of counsel. And for the present, adieu."

They went down towards the communicating door, and the Prince was left alone. He heard the door opened and closed, and silence fell upon the gardens save for the music of birds. For a few minutes he rested idly, with scarcely any connection of thought. The peace and quiet were inexpressibly pleasant to him. Presently he would read the letters once more.

Then he turned to what Ronnefeldt had said with so much emphasis. "If happiness should offer itself, as it certainly will, let no influence of the past hinder you from taking it." Here was the goodwill of a nature so strong that it would not easily be borne down by any hostile influence. Perhaps it could not understand men of a different fibre. How could a weaker man overcome the influences of a past like his, even if the word of forgiveness had been spoken? No sunshine of the present could disperse those shadows of a Fall, no music of birds or laughter of children could drown those mocking voices. And it was far, far more difficult here than in Waldington. There it had been possible to create a garden of illusion, a condition of things which for days and months had worn the appearance of reality and stability. Here every voice and every face was already a reminder, and there were others still more searching to be met in the to-morrows. That old Castle of Zell would have no disguise of alien towers when he went down to claim it, and the sword of the Hospodar would be as cumbrous and forbidding as ever. No, it would be better, much better, if he could be allowed to go away to build a new garden in some other Waldington, but a new garden more peaceful than the old because restitution had been made.

So he mused in his weakness, refusing to entertain the one thought which might have led him to the light. It stood at the threshold of his mind day and night, radiant with promise, but there was no hospitality for it in a heart so stricken and so timorous. So it had remained on the threshold, finding its opportunity only in his dreams. But in the morning he had always said, "It was a dream."

So he mused, while the birds sang and the autumn sun did its best to make an autumn summer; and when some ten minutes had passed he heard once more the sound of a closing door.

Was Ronnefeldt returning?

Chapter XXII

A Woman Takes an October Rose

IT was not the Chancellor. It was a woman who came to the junction of the paths and paused there to find her direction. Before she turned her face his heart had leaped to her name, and he was almost overwhelmed by an access of intense emotion. Joy, pain, fear seemed to come together in a flood, and he would have hidden himself. But there was no time, for she turned and saw him. She came towards the summer-house.

The Prince sat still. He could not rise to meet her. He thrust the joy away, for he saw that it was not his to take; pain and fear remained, the only guests with a right to stay. His conscience had dreaded the meeting with these women, for all manner of terrors surrounded it. Vaguely, yet reluctantly, he had hoped that it might be avoided. That lonely grave in Maywood Park—he would see it even through the pardon in their eyes. Then there were their months of pain in their London exile, and those other days when he had posed as their protector—he who had been at the very root of their troubles, whose identity had been a shame too dire to be revealed! No, he must not meet them, he could not face them.

But she was here, smiling as she approached, and apparently unsuspicious of his emotion. That was because there were shadows in the summer-house and she came through bright sunshine. She held out her hand, and he could not but take it; she took a chair and sat beside him, glowing with the beauty of a happy womanhood. Yes, she seemed to be happy, and not at all agitated at the meeting. To-day she wore light furs, open at the throat, and the furs harmonised with her hair and her colour. Certainly she was very beautiful—and it seemed clear that she would be kind.

"Do not move," she said gently. "I know you are weak still. The Chancellor said that I should find you here."

"Ronnefeldt sent you?" he asked.

"Yes. He said that you might see one of us, but not two. Mother will wait in his room till I return."

The first terror was over, and there had been little of terror after all. The Prince regained self-control in some measure. When he had done so, Joy looked in at the door, eager to enter; but Fear and Pain, though less imperious, refused to go.

"Your mother, I have heard, is well," he said.

"She is well and happy—yes, I think she is happy."

The cross in Maywood Park had shown itself for an instant, but vanished at once. "And I have come to thank you for her," added the girl. "Only a word, because I know I must not tire you."

Joy put a hesitant foot over the threshold.

"To thank me?" said the Prince. "You—to thank me?"

"Why, yes." The girl turned shining eyes upon
him. "That was why we came. We would have
written, but how could letters be enough?"

It was her look more than her words that gave
Fear and Pain their marching orders; but Joy was
not yet sure of her right.

"Oh, well," said the Prince. "You have been
too kind. Indeed, let me confess it—I was afraid
to meet you."

"Afraid?"

"Yes, afraid."

He tried to meet her eyes, but failed. At the
same moment he realised the Chancellor's kindness
in sending the girl instead of her mother. She was
of the new generation, to whom the infamy of
Adrian Zenandra was a shadowy, distant thing, and
to whom the services of James Herbertson were
real and immediate. But the Prince would have
no shirking of the truth.

"Yes," he said, "afraid. You know everything
now, and I have feared to meet you."

Then Rhona began to see the significance of
Ronnefeldt's words a few minutes ago. "Go and
see him," the Chancellor had said, "and tell him
what you think of him. Be sure to make him
understand." Rapidly she adjusted her thoughts
to this situation.

"Oh," she said softly. "I did not see how we
could think of you except in one way. Anything
else is impossible."

The Prince shook his head. How could he state
the case against himself? It did not need to be
stated. Reading his face, the girl felt her heart
stirred, for so much more of his amazing story

was revealed to her there. She had known it before, but now she realised it. And because she
saw an urgent need she resolved to meet it at any
cost. Very still and restrained was her tone.

"But we know all now," she said, "and we
still think the same. Shall I tell you what we
think?"

Still he could not face her, but there was something in her voice that banished Fear and Pain for
good. Joy came in and remained, sure of her
right.

"Please tell me," he said. "But be sure to
forget nothing."

There was a pause, while she conquered many
hesitancies and some conventions. These things
must be set aside in questions of life and death,
and she was strong enough to do it.

"We have reason to remember," she replied.
"Listen, then, while I tell you. There was a mere
boy to whom the perils of a high place came early,
before his character was established, before he had
time to discern the best things in life, or to exercise
the best traits in his own nature. He fell under the
influence of men who used him for their own ends,
able and astute men, sincere in their zeal but
unscrupulous. So he was lured from one step to
another, half dazzled, half in the dark, never being
allowed to see the truth. . . . But at last came the
day when he found that he had been guilty of what
were to his truly gentle nature the vilest of sins—
unfaith and ingratitude. And largely because his
nature had no coarseness in it, that knowledge
overwhelmed him, and he failed. Had he gone to
a true friend in that moment he would have been

saved, but the man who was nearest, though a faithful follower, was faint-hearted, and unequal to the crisis. He counselled flight, having no responsibility and failing to realise the seriousness of such a course. And before any true friend could intervene, the irrevocable step was taken and known to the world."

She paused. Her listener sat very still. . . . It seemed to be some fantastically new version of a terribly familiar story. She was not looking at him as she spoke. It needed a great effort to make the story clear.

"After many years," she went on, "he succeeded in burying and perhaps partly forgetting his shame. He lived a secure and quiet life then, filled with work, and kindness, and—yes—resignation. But in those years his true nature found itself, so that at last, when the need came, he was able to answer it, just as the old princes of his house answered the call of need in rougher days. But he did more than they, not less. They had died with the glory of the fight upon them, but he was willing to die without glory—a shameful, obscure and treacherous death at the hand of a hateful enemy. This he was willing to do so that he might atone for his great mistake; and in doing this, it seems to us, he proved himself a Prince indeed."

She paused again. How stifling was the beat of the heart in which Joy had taken up her abode, but how bewildering was the confusion of the mind! The Prince had to break the silence lest his heart should become audible.

"You have made something of me," he said.

"No," she replied. "Not I. It is as we see it,

but it is true. And I knew something of it when I saw you first, when you came to us in London with 'friend' upon your lips. I knew that our Deliverer had come. I cannot tell you how I knew it, but I did know it."

It was surely impossible to say more, but had she said enough? Did he understand? He sat so still, so downcast, so depressed. She was spurred to a few more words:

"That must have been why I never doubted your success," she said. "Do you remember what I told you?"

He looked up, and met her gaze: for having said all, she was brave enough to seal it by a look. The stars were bathed in dew, her cheeks were flushed, her lips were parted. Could he be mistaken in that look, reading it in the light of what she had just told him? Not mere gratitude, surely, could have moved her to think so, and to utter her thoughts so bravely. What could it be? And at the shock of the answer new life ran into his heart, bright vistas of hope, of happiness, opened before him. Loneliness—why, there could be no loneliness!

It was only for a moment, a magic moment; then the flood ebbed, the vision faded. He had made an absurd mistake. What he had imagined in her for that magic moment was all on his own side. It had helped to save him and restore him—he saw that clearly now—but that was all. Anything else was impossible!

So forgetting Ronnefeldt's last request he bowed under the shadow. "Ah," he said, covering his agitation with a great effort, "I thank you for those words. They are noble and generous. I am happy to know that you have both forgiven me."

She made no answer. What could she say more than she had said? Already, indeed, came the questionings of maidenly reserve, suggesting that she might have spoken too freely.

Too late—too late! In the moment of disillusionment he saw, some little distance off, a beautiful rose-bush just bursting into new bloom. He drew her attention to it.

"Look at that," he said. "It is coming into bloom just as the frosts are approaching to destroy it. It is a foolish thing that flowers so late in the year."

Naturally she failed to take his meaning upon the instant, quick though her instincts were; and, while she tried to understand, they heard a sound of footsteps.

"It is my servant," he said. "I told him to come here for me." And she rose.

"I fear that I have been here too long," she said.

"Not too long," he protested; and as he spoke he saw how joy must go with her, and the whole world was as grey as his face. But there could be nothing else for him, and he rose to say good-bye. "But some day," he said, "we shall meet again."

"Yes," she replied. "Some day."

Then she gave him her hand, once more looking into his face. She saw there how the old mood had overwhelmed him, the old diffidence and self-distrust; she understood his bitter parable, and at the same moment she recalled the definite emphasis of the Chancellor's words—*make him understand.* But what more could she do? And seeing that she could do nothing, she smiled a little sadly, and turned, and walked down the broad path that would take her away from him for ever.

But Fortune and Destiny lingered in that path, awaiting fulfilment and opportunity; and at that instant Fortuna bestirred herself, for she heard the footsteps of Nemesis following hard upon this poor man's lack of assurance. So as Rhona came to a certain rose-bush, a magic breeze sighed through the garden and stirred its branches, so that the fairest of its blossoms caught her attention. It was the bush of which he had spoken, and when she saw it a great thought came to her. For the Prince, watching her, saw that she paused, full in his sight, beside the bush, and plucked that blossom, and kissed it, and set it in her bosom. Then for a moment she stood, looking back at him bravely and not ashamed of what she had done. After that she passed on.

But he understood. His heart thundered, his visions returned, he saw that from the beginning everything had been drawing to this end. He was not old, and his love was sufficiently young and strong to soar to the great stars and to look death in the face. He saw that Ronnefeldt, the omniscient Ronnefeldt, had read him from the first, and had guessed what power it was that had brought him back from the dead. And it was Ronnefeldt that had sent her here this morning, after begging him to accept the happiness that would certainly offer itself. Had Ronnefeldt read the woman's heart as well as the man's?

His servant was now close at hand. "Go," he cried hoarsely. "Call her—ask her to come back."

The man made haste.   He overtook her and delivered his message just as she reached the door. Not for a moment did she hesitate, but came back, with her eyes full of the light that should be the glory of the days to come.   The man did not follow her, but remained at the door.

The Prince stood back from the threshold, leaning against a table.   Even now he was afraid, and faint from the tumult of his emotions.   He looked at her with a momentous question that woke in her heart something of the eternal mother that is in every woman, so that she was obliged to answer once and for ever.   She came near, slowly, until he knew the fragrance of her breath and her hair. She raised her hands to his shoulders, and she whispered "My Prince!"   Then she lifted her face for that first kiss which is the Paradise of every lover.

THE  END